# REASON AND CONDUCT
## IN
# HUME'S TREATISE

# REASON AND CONDUCT
## IN
# HUME'S TREATISE

BY

RACHAEL M. KYDD

*NEW YORK*

RUSSELL & RUSSELL · INC

1964

FIRST PUBLISHED IN 1946
REISSUED, 1964, BY RUSSELL & RUSSELL, INC.
L. C. CATALOG CARD NO: 64—11846

PRINTED IN THE UNITED STATES OF AMERICA

# PREFACE

IN recent years there has been a great revival of interest in Hume's philosophy. This interest is, however, largely confined to his epistemology. It would not be true to say that his moral and practical philosophy are totally ignored, for they receive considerable attention in both Professor Laird's[1] and Professor Kemp Smith's[2] accounts of his philosophy, but, with the exception of a short work by Ingemar Hedenius[3] and Miss Shearer's Bryn Mawr thesis,[4] the present century has seen no whole book devoted to this aspect of his work. Thus it might well be argued that there is great need for a comprehensive examination of that part of Hume's philosophy which is comprised in the second and third books of the *Treatise of Human Nature* and in the *Inquiry Concerning Morals*. The present book has no such ambitious aspiration. It is not an exhaustive exposition and examination of the whole of this part of Hume's philosophy, nor even of a very considerable part of it. It is, indeed, concerned with no more than a fraction of his total ethical writings. More than half of what follows is confined to two short sections of the *Treatise*, the sections 'Of the Influencing Motives of the Will' and 'Moral Distinctions not Derived from Reason'; the rest is concerned with some of Hume's remarks in the sections about the 'calm and violent passions' and in those about the 'artificial virtues'. There are also, in the sixth chapter, some references to the sections about the 'natural virtues'. Throughout I have considered only those passages which have a direct bearing on a very limited problem: the relation between reason and action. Moreover, the interest of this thesis is not primarily historical, for it is not about Hume as a writer on reason and action, but about reason and action in so far as they are considered by Hume. I am not concerned with this problem because it was, among others, one which Hume discussed, but because it is in itself a problem of great

---

[1] *Hume's Philosophy of Human Nature.*      [2] *The Philosophy of David Hume.*
[3] *Studies in Hume's Ethics.*      [4] *Hume's Place in Ethics.*

philosophical interest and Hume's contribution to its solution is very considerable.

The importance of this part of Hume's philosophy, and indeed the importance of the problem of reason and action as a whole, has in the main been disregarded by modern moralists. And yet we must conclude that Hume was right in thinking that it is a problem which is most fundamental to moral philosophy. Can reason influence conduct? Upon our answer to this depends our answer to the further question, Are moral judgements possible? If reason cannot influence conduct then we cannot argue about morality; and the ways in which we can argue about morality are dependent upon what kinds of judgement can influence action.

That this is so is not at present generally realized, yet it follows as readily from the premises accepted by modern moralists as from those which were current in the early eighteenth century. It is, I think, generally agreed that the fundamental, if not the only, problem of moral philosophy is that of *duty* or *obligation*. It is true that many moralists are also concerned with *rightness* and *goodness*, but I think that this concern is rooted in the view that it is the rightness or goodness of acts which constitutes their obligatoriness. Take away the concept of obligation and there would be no moral philosophy. Further, with regard to obligation two premises are generally, though sometimes tacitly, accepted; the first that men cannot be obliged to do acts which they cannot do—'ought' implies 'can'—and the second that it is impossible to act without a motive. The latter premiss is not so widely accepted as the former, yet it, too, seems to be valid and indeed it is implied by any plausible definition of action. From these two premises it follows that we cannot be obliged to do acts which we have no motive to do, and hence that the discovery that an act is an obligation must, *inter alia*, always be the discovery of a *motive for acting*. From this Hume in his time concluded that moral judgements, if there be any, must be practical.

Hence the problem whether reason can be practical, that is to say whether an agent can make judgements which provide him with a motive for acting, rests at the very heart of moral philosophy. If reason were impotent in this respect there would be no moral judgements. Neither would there be any moral philosophy. There might indeed remain a science devoted to moral beliefs, but this science could only be concerned with their description and explanation and not with their validity: it would, therefore, be more properly classed as psychology than as philosophy. We would not be able to think, to argue, to be mistaken, or to change our minds about our obligations; and this situation would be disastrous not merely for moral philosophy but for common morality as well.

Yet modern moralists do not seem to be aware of this fact. While maintaining, on the one hand, that 'ought' implies 'can' and that 'can' implies a motive, they assume, on the other, that we can make judgements, and even *a priori* judgements, about our obligations. Yet they make no attempt to establish the compatibility of these two assertions by showing how judgements can give rise to motivation. Hume, on the other hand, considered this problem carefully, and for this reason his arguments are of more than historical interest. They would, indeed, be interesting as a link between the early eighteenth century and Kant, even if post-Kantian philosophers had accepted them to the extent to which Kant himself did, and if they were now a commonplace of ethics. But this is so far from being the case that we have still not only to learn about Hume but also to learn from him.

Not all this book is therefore strictly concerned with reason and conduct. It has been necessary to consider also the place that this problem occupies in Hume's moral philosophy; it is with this question that Chapters II and VI are concerned. I have also found it necessary to say something about the seventeenth- and eighteenth-century background to Hume's treatment of the problem, and this I have done in Chapter I. This chapter is, however, of necessity long, for, since the works with which it deals are neither well known nor easily obtainable, it has often been necessary to quote at length passages which might otherwise have been passed with a mere reference.

Moreover, the light which it throws on Hume's treatment of
our problem is historical rather than philosophical. Those who
are interested only in Hume should omit it, and those whose
interest is strictly confined to Hume's analysis of the influence of reason on conduct, the proper subject of this book,
should omit Chapters II and VI as well.

I have to acknowledge my debt to my supervisor Mr. W. D.
Falk for first calling my attention to Hume's contribution in
this field. I had originally intended to analyse Spinoza's theory
of the relation between reason and the affections, a theory in
many respects very similar to Hume's, together with that of
the relation between reason and morality. But it soon became
evident that it was not possible to examine this part of Spinoza's
doctrine in isolation from his theory of knowledge, on the one
hand, and his account of the relation between mind and body
on the other. It was clear that the work involved would be on
too ambitious a scale. In these circumstances Mr. Falk called
my attention to the fact that many of the problems which
interested me in the later books of the *Ethics* received a similar
treatment in the second and third books of the *Treatise*. I am
indebted to him also on more consequential grounds. For it
is to him I owe the whole approach to moral philosophy and
to the relation between reason and moral conduct which under-
lies my interpretation of the passages here examined. In view
of the fact that, with the exception of two articles in *Philosophy*,[1]
none of Mr. Falk's work has yet been published I am anxious
fully to acknowledge my indebtedness. When I first came to
discuss with him the problems of moral philosophy I found
that all the main principles of a view towards which I was
naturally very sympathetic, but of which I had only certain
vague conceptions, were already carefully formulated. For me
it remained only to work out certain details and to apply these
principles to the interpretation of Hume's theory. I should
like to thank him, also, for his patience in reading many successive drafts of the whole book and for making many

[1] 'Morals without Faith', *Philosophy*, April, 1944; 'Obligation and Rightness',
*Philosophy*, July, 1945.

invaluable suggestions, particularly about the order of the argument. My thanks are due also to Mrs. Kneale for reading all six chapters and making many valuable suggestions. Also to Professor Paton for reading all the proofs and calling my attention to many inaccuracies which I had overlooked. Such errors and omissions as remain are due entirely to my own perversity.

Finally I have to thank Mrs. Warne for her great help in typing the manuscript.

All references to the *Treatise of Human Nature* are to the Everyman edition.

This book is dedicated to my father.

R. M. K.

OXFORD
*February*, 1945.

# CONTENTS

# CHAPTER I

## HUME'S PREDECESSORS

AT the beginning of the seventeenth century Herbert of Cherbury wrote his celebrated book *De Veritate*, and there we find the following passage:

'It is of the highest importance to distinguish these Common Notions [of Morality] and to allot each of these indubitable truths to its proper position. This has never been so necessary as now. For men are now not only exhorted by every device that language can employ by arguments from the pulpit, but are tormented in spite of the protests of conscience and the inner consciousness, by the belief that all who are outside their particular Church are condemned, whether through ignorance or error, to undergo . . . eternal punishment after death. The wretched terror-stricken mass have no refuge, unless some immovable foundations of truth resting on universal consent are established, to which they can turn amid the doubts of theology or of philosophy. . . . They have no criterion, but dully immersing themselves in a naïve credulity, they become incapable of using their own faculties; and not having the heart to confront the terrors with which they are threatened, they fall back on fear and hate.'[1]

It was thus that Herbert described the urgency of the problem which nearly all his successors down to the middle of the eighteenth century tried to solve, the problem of how to establish the validity of moral propositions and hence the laws of morality.

The need to find a solution to this problem arose from the emergence of different religious sects at the Reformation. During the Middle Ages the question had little practical importance, and this was due not so much to the universal acceptance of revelation as the arbiter of moral conduct, as to the uniformity of the precepts that were adopted. So long as the moral code promulgated by the Catholic Church was generally adhered to it was a matter of indifference for practical purposes whether this code was established by reason or by faith. Popular morality was no doubt a matter of faith; moral acts

---

[1] Herbert of Cherbury, *De Veritate*, Carré edition, p. 117.

were those which received the sanction of the Church and their morality rested on its authority. That is not to say that philosophers were unconcerned with the problem of demonstrating moral propositions. Thomas Aquinas, like many others, regarded the truth of such propositions as made evident by the light of reason. All knowledge of morality was, he maintained, derived from the two premisses: 'Bona sunt sequenda, mala vitanda', premisses which, he thought, shared the status of the law of contradiction. Yet the question of how moral judgements were possible was not regarded as of primary importance even by philosophers, nor was it responsible for any of the great medieval controversies. This apathy towards moral problems was no doubt due to the fact that no practical matters were involved in their solution. For philosophical disquisitions on moral laws were not likely either to increase or decrease adherence to them. Such adherence was already assured by the general acceptance of the Church's unrivalled authority.

With the Reformation came a great change, a change due not so much to the breakdown of faith as such as to the division of authority. The different religious sects accepted different interpretations of the holy text making it no longer possible to claim that authority alone was the arbiter of moral conduct. This development did not entail the complete rejection of the view that morality was revealed, but it necessitated the establishing of some criterion by which to distinguish genuine from false revelation; and, so far as morals were concerned, the view was generally accepted that God revealed those laws which were themselves agreeable to reason.

Thus arose the necessity which Herbert describes of showing how reason can discover the truth of moral propositions and of establishing by its means fundamental moral principles to which all could agree. The problem in which the medievals had only an academic interest acquired at the Reformation an immense practical significance. It was this practical significance which in its turn stimulated widespread philosophical inquiry, so that, by the seventeenth century, ethical questions rivalled logical and metaphysical ones as the centre of philo-

sophical controversy. It would not be true to say that all
philosophers were concerned with morals, nor even that all who
wrote about morals argued in favour of the rational verification
of moral propositions; there remained many who maintained
that revelation was the final arbiter of moral conduct,[1] and
others, sceptics who like Bayle,[2] Rochefoucault, and later,
Mandeville mistrusted faith, but were equally depreciative of
reason and concluded that no moral laws could properly be
established. Furthermore, not all those who sought a solution
to this problem did so to the exclusion of others. Nevertheless
it is true to say that the attempts to solve it were many and form
the great bulk of the moral philosophy of the period.

Some familiarity with these attempts is a necessary prerequisite to the understanding of those parts of Hume's philosophy
that are examined in the rest of this book. The last part of the
second book of the *Treatise* and the first part of the third are
concerned with the problem of rationalism in ethics and are
best understood as a critique of the earlier attempts to establish
the relation between reason and morality. We must, therefore,
begin with a survey of Hume's predecessors not in order that
we may discover the particular influence of various philosophers on Hume—we are not looking for the historical sources
of his philosophy—but so that we may lay bare the fundamental
tendencies in a chain of philosophical argument which culminated in the *Treatise*, and become familiar with those controversies which in some degree the *Treatise* solved.

We have said that the greater part of seventeenth- and early

---

[1] See, for instance, Jeremy Taylor, *The Rule of Conscience*, 4th edition, 1696,
p. 177, where he writes of the Laws of Nature: 'Practical reason or conscience
is its record, but revelation and express declaring it, was the first publication
and emission of it, and till then it had not all the solemnities of law. . . .'

[2] See *Dictionary*, English translation, vol. i, p. 75, footnote G: 'Let the
matter be how it will, there is no man that makes use of his reason, but has
need of the assistance of God, without which 'tis a guide that leads us astray.
And we may compare philosophy to certain powders so very corrosive, that
having consumed the proud and spongious flesh of a wound, they would eat
up the quick and sound flesh, rot the bones, and pierce to the very marrow.
Philosophy is proper at first to confute errors, but if she be not stopped there,
she attacks truth it self; and when she has her full scope, she goes so far that
she loses her self, and knows not where to rest.'

eighteenth-century moral philosophy was devoted to answering
the question: How can reason verify moral propositions?
Nearly all agreed that reason could verify such propositions,
but to the question, How can it verify them? their answers
were widely different. These differences were due to divergent
opinions about both the objects of moral propositions and the
nature of rational proof—and, we may add, the study of their
answers is not made easier by the fact that disagreement on
these two questions was often only implicit. It is important
to note, however, that in this latter respect the seventeenth
and eighteenth centuries were not alike. Among seventeenth-
century philosophers we find few who offer any explicit definition of either the object of moral propositions or the nature of
rational proof, and few who are even consistent in the definitions
which they implicitly allot to them. By the eighteenth century
this is no longer the case. Each philosopher attributes, although
again often implicitly, a more or less precise meaning to each of
these terms, but here the meanings vary considerably with each
philosopher. Thus we can say that the evolution of the problem was as follows: First philosophers became aware of the
practical need to find some basis of morality other than revelation, and they looked for this basis in reason. But in tackling
the problem of showing how reason can be the basis of morality
they failed to make clear to themselves from the outset either
the precise nature of the propositions which reason was required to prove or what sort of rational proof was needed.
Such was the state of confusion in which the problem was left
at the turn of the century. But in the years that followed
philosophers began to approach this problem with a clearer
notion of the issues involved.

Let us consider first the seventeenth-century views of the
nature of moral propositions. Obligation, rightness, goodness,
justice, honour, and virtue have all at different times and by
different philosophers been regarded as the proper objects of
moral propositions. There is no prima-facie objection to such
usages, but if we are to consider the kinds of verifications of

which moral propositions are susceptible it is necessary to know to which of the above things they are supposed to refer. It may indeed well be that propositions about all of them are capable of the same sort of proof, but this is itself a philosophical problem. It is strictly illegitimate, for example, to show that propositions about rightness allow of one sort of verification and then to assume that propositions about obligation can be similarly verified for no other reason than that we began by classing both as moral propositions—unless indeed the words 'right' and 'obligatory' are used strictly as synonyms. Yet this is exactly the kind of argument that we find in the writings of nearly all seventeenth-century moralists. Herbert of Cherbury, for instance, confuses good and obligatory in this way. He refers to good acts and obligatory acts as moral, shows that propositions about the goodness of acts can be verified in one way,[1] and then assumes without further proof that what he had said about propositions attributing goodness applies equally to propositions attributing obligatoriness.[2] Yet there can be no doubt that by an act's 'being good' and its 'being an obligation' he understands two quite different predications. That the proposition 'doing good acts is obligatory' is never supposed by him to be a tautology is evident from his assertion that men 'ought not to act evilly for they are not enjoined to do so by Common Notions'.[3] He falls into this error simply because he uses the word 'moral' indiscriminately.

A similar confusion occurs in Grotius, but, whereas Herbert fails to distinguish clearly between good and obligatory, Grotius confuses right and obligatory. '*Jus*', he writes, 'has a third signification, meaning Law in its largest sense, namely, "a rule of moral acts obliging to what is right".'[4] We cannot say that all seventeenth-century philosophers are guilty of such confusion. Pufendorf, for example, is perfectly consistent in his use of terms. He treats moral propositions as concerned only with obligation, and although he uses the words 'good' and 'just' he uses them as synonyms for 'obligatory' and never

---

[1] *De Veritate*, p. 184.    [2] Ibid., p. 193.    [3] Ibid., p. 192.
[4] Grotius, *Rights of Peace and War*, translated Whewell, 1853, p. 3; see also p. 9.

to denote any further characteristic. They mean 'in accordance
with moral law'. We are not obliged to do acts because they
are good and just, but we call them good and just because we
are obliged to do them.[1] Thus in so far as he succeeds in
showing how propositions about one of these terms can be
verified, what he has shown applies *ipso facto* to the verification
of propositions about them all. In fact Pufendorf criticizes
Grotius for saying that acts are obligatory because they are
right—though apparently without recognizing that Grotius
understands by 'rightness' and 'obligation' two quite separate
characteristics, for he ascribes Grotius's error to circular
argument:

'. . . if the definition of Natural Law is to be founded on that necessary
honesty or turpitude of some actions, it must be always perplex'd and
obscure, and run round in an unconcluding circle; as will appear to
any man who examines the definition laid down by Grotius.'[2]

We may say that Pufendorf is mistaken in this criticism in so
far as he considers that Grotius means by 'rightness' and
'obligation' one and the same thing; yet he is justified in
assuming this to be Grotius's meaning by the fact that Grotius
ignores the question: Why are right acts obligatory? a question
to which some answer would be required if he distinguished
the two concepts. Yet again, we may argue, this criticism is
valid only against one of Grotius's definitions, for there are
many.

It is not possible to consider the degree to which all, or even
many, seventeenth-century philosophers are guilty of substi-
tuting one 'moral term' for another and assuming that what
had been proved of one is true *ipso facto* of the other. Not all
are guilty in the same degree. Pufendorf, as we have seen, is
exempt, and certainly Shaftesbury is less guilty than Grotius,

---

[1] *The Law of Nature and of Nations*, English transl. Oxford, 1703, pp. 60,
61, 62.
[2] Ibid., p. 95; see also p. 46. 'As to Grotius's definition, where he says the
law obligeth to that which is right, we must observe, he supposeth somewhat
to be just and right before any rule or law; whence it must follow that the law
of nature doth not make what we call right, but only denotes or points it out
as a thing already existent.'

Hobbes than Malebranche; and in many, as in Cumberland,[1] the confusion of words is superficial and does not affect the substance of their argument. Yet there can be no doubt that there was a great confusion, and one which, in the eighteenth century, became responsible for much philosophical contention.

I began by saying that the seventeenth-century conception of the rational verification of moral propositions was ambiguous on two grounds; of these it was the second ambiguity, that concerning the nature of rational verification, which led to the more complicated if not to the more serious confusions. I do not know of any seventeenth-century philosopher, with the sole exception of Spinoza, who gives an explicit answer to the question: What constitutes rational proof when applied to moral propositions? And the answers which they give implicitly—what each takes to constitute such rational proof—vary considerably even in the works of one and the same philosopher.

Roughly we can say that there were three separate conceptions of rational proof, though each of these was subject to variations. An act was said to be obligatory, or right, or good, as the case might be, (i) If the proposition asserting it to be so was a tautology: it was a common variation of this view that an act was wrong, or one which rational beings were obliged to refrain from doing, not when the proposition about it, but when the act itself, was contrary to the laws of logic. (ii) If the proposition asserting the act to be right or obligatory was such as could be seen to be self-evidently true not because it was a tautology but because it agreed with an innate idea. This view varied with the view taken of innate ideas. (iii) If the act could be shown to agree with the nature of man. It is clear that on either of the first two theories moral propositions are capable of *a priori* verification whereas on the third they

---

[1] Pufendorf writes of Cumberland as not falling into Grotius's confusion. See ibid., p. 95. But he himself is not wholly free from obscurity on this question.

admit of empirical verification only. But an additional complication is introduced by the fact that those moralists who adopt the third kind of proof, equally with those who adopt the first two, refer to moral propositions as *necessarily* true and to moral laws as *eternal* and *immutable*. This they do despite the fact that they derive these laws entirely from the nature and conditions of man, that is, from empirical premisses.

These differences in the conceptions of rational proof had serious consequences mainly because their acceptance was to a large degree implicit. Philosophers not only argued at cross purposes with one another, but one and the same philosopher adopted different conceptions of proof. Frequently the first and the third, sometimes the first and the second, were employed indiscriminately. This led to serious difficulties, for, since it cannot be shown *a priori* that the two classes of acts derived from the application of these two criteria must coincide, those who employ them are always in danger of discovering, not one single self-consistent system of moral laws but a dichotomy. Whenever two supreme principles are applied it is always possible that men will be faced with conflicting duties and be without any final criterion by which to distinguish between them.

The view that a moral proposition is proved true when it has been shown that an act is intrinsically reasonable was, as we have already hinted, itself a complex view. Acts, it was argued, are moral, not only when *propositions* asserting their *morality* agree with the laws of logic, but also when their *occurrence* itself is compatible with reason and when their omission would itself be self-contradictory. This view was carried to its logical conclusion by Wollaston in the eighteenth century, yet it was held in some degree by many seventeenth-century philosophers—though it is, I think, true to say that none of them held it to the exclusion of other views. Normally it was held together with the empiricist theory that acts are recognized as moral when they are seen to be conducive to the good, or happiness, or preservation of the agent.

Grotius, Hobbes, and Pufendorf are all mainly concerned

with empirical proof, but they all at times adopt the *a priori* method. Thus Grotius writes that the principle of self-pre-servation commends us to right reason, but adds that '. . . right reason ought to be dearer to us than those things by which we were first led to use it'.[1] Similarly Pufendorf maintains that the 'dictates of right reason are true principles, which agree with the nature of things well observ'd and examin'd; and which are deduc'd from other true and first principles, by the rules of good consequence'.[2] And Hobbes, in a well-known passage which is quite incompatible with the rest of his philo-sophy, seriously contends that immoral action is logically self-contradictory: 'There is', he writes, 'a great similitude between what we call *injury*, or *injustice*, in the actions and conversations of men in the world, and that which is called *absurd* in the arguments and disputations of the Schools. . . . There is in every breach of covenant a contradiction properly so called.' He goes on to argue, though without any plausibility, that to break a promise is to will the doing and not doing of the same thing at the same time, which, he says, is 'plain contradiction', and he concludes: 'Injury is an absurdity of conversation, as absurdity is a kind of injustice in disputation.'[3]

The predication of 'reasonable' to acts, meaning 'compatible with the laws of logic', seems to have resulted from transference of the epithet 'reasonable' from the proposition asserting the possibility of acts to the acts themselves. A similar transference was made by Malebranche, who referred not simply to *acts* as reasonable but also to *things*, and acts he thought were reason-able in so far as they agreed with the 'reason of things'.

I have said that those who held this view never held it by itself. Even Malebranche meant by a 'reasonable act' two distinctly different things. Sometimes he uses 'reasonable' to describe an act which is in accordance with the 'reason of things' and which it would be logically impossible to omit, sometimes simply to describe that act which promotes the good

---

[1] *Rights of Peace and War*, p. 9.
[2] *Law of Nature and of Nations*, p. 105.
[3] *De Corpore Politico*, in *Hobbes Tripos*, London, 1840, p. 96.

of the agent. Yet although such use of the word 'reasonable' is confusing, it does not in Malebranche lead to a dichotomy of duties, for he maintains that doing acts which are reasonable in the first sense is *ipso facto* doing those which are reasonable in the second; for acting in accordance with the 'reason of things' leads necessarily to the agent's true good, since by so doing he avoids the punishments of hell and reaps instead the rewards of heaven.[1] For Pufendorf, Grotius, and Hobbes, on the other hand, the use of both empirical and *a priori* criteria results in serious difficulties since none offers any explanation of why the two classes of moral acts thus derived should coincide. It might be that acting in the self-contradictory manner described by Hobbes—if indeed this were possible—would lead to the self-destruction or misery of the agent, but there is no prima-facie reason why this should be so, and the *onus probandi* rests with them. Yet clearly all are unaware of this difficulty. As we have seen they all at times adopted the *a priori* view, yet they all also speak of moral acts as reasonable in the sense of being those of which reason discovers that they promote the true good of the agent. Thus Grotius writes:

'. . . in as much as man is superior to other animals . . . in his judgement and power of estimating advantages and disadvantages; and in these, not only present good and ill, but also future good and ill, and what may lead to each; we may understand that it is congruous to human nature to follow, in such matters . . . a judgement rightly framed; not to be misled by fear or by the temptation of present pleasure, nor to be carried away by blind and thoughtless impulse; and that what is plainly repugnant to such judgement, is also contrary to *Jus*, that is, to Natural Human Law.'[2]

A very similar passage occurs in Hobbes's *De Corpore*:

'Reason is no less of the nature of man than passion, and is the same in all men, because all men agree in the will to be directed and governed in the way to that which they desire to attain, namely their own good, which is the work of reason: there can therefore be no other law of nature than reason.'[3]

---

[1] See his *Treatise of Morality*, trans. James Shipton, 1699.
[2] *Rights of Peace and War*, p. xxv.
[3] *De Corpore Politico*, p. 87; see also p. 109: 'Every man by natural passion,

We turn now from those who hold that reason can make moral judgements *a priori* because the morality of an act consists in its agreement with the laws of logic, to those who contend that moral judgements are certain because of the morality of actions men have innate ideas. These philosophers also, in some degree, maintain an empiricist position side by side with this *a priori* one.[1] Their main contention is that moral propositions are self-evident, but their self-evidence is divorced from logical necessity; we recognize their truth by inspection without formal proof. For Herbert of Cherbury innate ideas and logical deduction both play some part; we have Common Notions of our general duties, and our particular duties are deduced from these by our conscience,[2] but it is on innate ideas that he bases his moral theory. This view of moral judgements was not held so widely as what might be called the analytic view: it seems on the whole to have been confined to Herbert and certain Cambridge Platonists.[3]

The precise nature of innate ideas or Common Notions is never clearly defined, but evidently Herbert's meaning is very different from Descartes's. Sometimes by Common Notions he seems to mean merely those notions which are common to all—if this were his meaning he could not argue that on this ground men have *a priori* knowledge of particular duties—but his more usual view is that Common Notions are those to which all, after merely inspecting them, must give their consent.[4] This view is, we have said, presented side by side with the ordinary empirical arguments. Herbert, like Hobbes and Grotius, maintains that we know that an act is moral when we recognize that it would promote our good. 'Put your faith

calleth that good which pleaseth him for the present . . . and in like manner, that which displeaseth him, evil. And therefore he that foreseeth the whole way to his preservation, which is the end that every one by nature aimeth at, must also call it good, and the contrary evil. And this is that good and evil, which not every man in passion calleth so, but all men by reason.'

[1] No arguments from innate ideas are to be found in the works of Hobbes, Grotius, Pufendorf, and Cumberland. The last two explicitly reject this view.

[2] *De Veritate*, p. 116 and p. 186.

[3] See, for instance, Cudworth, *Concerning Immutable and Unalterable Morality*, p. 287.

[4] *De Veritate*, p. 140.

in Common Notions, they provide a way which cannot deceive us for they lead straight to happiness.'[1] It is true that, for Herbert, as for Malebranche, the acceptance of these two criteria does not lead to a dichotomy of moral laws, for he maintains that acting in accordance with Common Notions leads to our happiness; God has specially given us these notions so that we shall do that which is for our own true good.[2] Yet he never proves that this is so, and if some perverse individual were to maintain that acting in accordance with Common Notions was contrary to his true happiness, Herbert would provide him with no criterion by which to distinguish whether the act conducive to his happiness or the act which agreed with Common Notions was that which he really ought to do.

We have said that the majority of seventeenth-century moralists, having in fact used both *a priori* and empirical reasoning to verify moral propositions, added further confusion by claiming that their empirical arguments as well as their *a priori* ones were demonstrative. Grotius himself distinguishes between *a priori* and *a posteriori* proof, but that which he describes as *a priori* is plainly empirical. Of Natural Law he writes that it is commonly proved in both ways:

'It is proved *a priori* by shewing the agreement or disagreement of anything with the rational and social nature of man. It is proved *a posteriori* when by certain or very probable accounts we find anything accepted as Natural Law among all nations, or at least the more civilized.'[3]

He fails to recognize that man's social nature is an empirical fact and is not definitive of man, and that consequently the proposition which asserts the authority of natural laws for all men is, in so far as it rests on this premiss, also an empirical proposition. Grotius is so far from observing this that he emphasizes the eternal and immutable character of the laws derived from man's empirical nature:

'Natural Law', he writes, 'is so immutable that it cannot be changed by God himself. For though the power of God be immense, there are

---

[1] *De Veritate*, pp. 135, 126.        [2] Ibid., p. 190.
[3] *Rights of Peace and War*, p. 5.

some things to which it does not extend: because if we speak of these things being done, the words are mere words, and have no meaning, being self-contradictory. Thus God himself cannot make twice two not be four; and in like manner, he cannot make that which is intrinsically bad, not be bad. For as the essence of things, when they exist . . . does not depend on anything else, so it is with the properties which follow that essence: and such a property is the baseness of certain actions, when compared with the nature of rational beings.'[1]

This statement clearly refers to moral rules which he thinks are known *a priori* because they agree, not with the laws of logic, but with the nature of man. It is interesting to notice that Grotius was criticized on this account by Jeremy Taylor, who points out that the Laws of Nature are relative to given states of affairs and adds, '. . . therefore it is unwarily said of the learned Hugo Grotius, and of divers others before him, that God cannot change the Law of Nature'.[2] Yet Pufendorf, Cumberland, and even Shaftesbury were guilty of the same error.[3]

Of all the seventeenth-century moralists who argued that moral propositions are capable of demonstration it was undoubtedly Locke whose influence was greatest in the succeeding century. Locke, however, unlike Grotius and Pufendorf, did not proffer an *a priori* moral theory because he confused empirical and *a priori* proof. The propositions which he cites in the section entitled 'Morality Capable of Demonstration' are certainly *a priori*. 'Where there is no property', he writes, 'there is no justice', and 'No government allows of absolute liberty'.[4] But, though these propositions are *a priori*, they are certainly not *moral* in any of the senses in which 'moral' was used in the seventeenth and early eighteenth centuries. They do not assert that an act is right, or good, or obligatory, or even

[1] Ibid., p. 4.  [2] *The Rule of Conscience*, p. 181.
[3] See Pufendorf, *Law of Nature and of Nations*, p. 106, &c. And Cumberland, *A Treatise on the Laws of Nature*, trans. Maxwell, 1727, p. 39, where he refers to the Laws of Nature as 'propositions of unchangeable truth'. And Shaftesbury, *Inquiry Concerning Virtue*, p. 197, '. . . so that the method taken may perhaps for this reason be call'd a sort of *Moral Arithmetic*, and be said to have an evidence as great as may be found in numbers, and equal to Mathematical Demonstration.'
[4] *Essay Concerning the Human Understanding*, Pringle Pattison, p. 277.

that an agent is good or virtuous. Moreover, it is to be doubted whether Locke ever seriously intended to maintain that genuine moral propositions could be demonstrably verified. Earlier in the *Essay* he seems to regard them as empirical; thus, under the heading 'Faith and Justice not Owned by All Men', he writes: 'Whether there be any such moral principles wherein all men do agree, I appeal to any who have been but moderately conversant in the history of mankind, and looked abroad beyond the smoke of their own chimneys.'[1]

When we turn from the seventeenth to the early eighteenth century we find a considerable change in the philosophical treatment both of the nature of moral propositions and of their rational verification. Roughly, this change can be described by saying that each philosopher tends to adopt only one view on each of these questions. With regard to the first, it would certainly not be true to say that each, or indeed any, offers an explicit definition of a moral proposition nor even that a precise and unambiguous meaning is implicit in their works; but we can say that some definitions are implied, and further that during the first three decades the usages of some philosophers came to be recognized by others as the source of what they considered a mistaken philosophy. Thus, by the time that Hume wrote the *Treatise* the nature of moral propositions was already a bone of contention and the problem of their content was, in some degree, recognized as a philosophical problem. With regard to rational proof, here too it gradually became evident that the *a priori* and empirical methods were not equally applicable; some philosophers adopted the one method, some the other, but we find few who continue to use both indiscriminately. And as the century progressed the question of what kind of verification could best be applied to moral propositions, like the question of their content, came to be recognized as a problem, and it also formed the ground of philosophical argument. Finally, confusions about the difference between

---

[1] *Essay Concerning the Human Understanding*, p. 28. See also *Treatise of Civil Government*, the chapter on the State of Nature, where he puts forward empirical arguments for the morality of certain acts.

empirical and *a priori* arguments did not persist into the eighteenth century—we no longer find inferences drawn from empirical premisses described as necessarily true propositions.

The moral philosophers of the early eighteenth century can be divided into different schools according to their view of the nature of moral propositions, and according to their conception of the manner in which these propositions are verified. On the application of each principle they fall into two schools of thought; on the first, into those who mean by 'moral' primarily 'right' and 'fitting', and those who mean 'obligatory'; and, on the second, into those who maintain that propositions attributing moral characteristics are demonstrable, and those who consider that they are capable of empirical verification only. But these two principles of division do not yield four different schools of thought which might be called, 'rightness *a priori*', 'rightness empirical', 'obligation *a priori*', 'obligation empirical'. Nearly all those who use 'moral' to mean 'right' maintain that moral propositions are demonstrable, and all who use 'moral' to mean 'obligatory'—with the notable exception of Wollaston—regard them as empirical.

We must now consider these two schools of thought in some detail, for it was in opposition to those who maintained, on the one hand, that moral propositions are concerned with rightness and fittingness, and, on the other, that they can be capable of demonstration, that Hume developed his arguments against moral rationalism.

At the beginning of the eighteenth century there was a great number of philosophers and theologians who, following up one aspect of Cumberland's philosophy,[1] implicitly maintained that *rightness* or *fittingness* is the main concern of moral philosophers.[2] That moral propositions are concerned with the rightness of actions is itself an ambiguous statement. In the

[1] Cumberland, of course, did not on the whole maintain this view at all, but there are several isolated passages where he at least assumes that moral propositions are about fittingness, which seems to indicate that he held this view together with others, though the others are responsible for the more interesting parts of his philosophy.

[2] Of these the best known was Samuel Clarke and the most philosophical John Balguy.

seventeenth century no attempts were made to define 'right'. Grotius at times uses it as synonymous with just and honourable, and Cumberland as synonymous with fitting; but these philosophers had only a vague conception of the term. The early eighteenth-century moralists, on the other hand, try to analyse rightness, and it was to this attempt that Samuel Clarke owed his widespread contemporary influence in the eighteenth century as well as such popularity as he enjoys to-day. In fact, a close examination of his views leaves more bewilderment than illumination, yet since they led to a controversy which culminated in the *Treatise*, and with which we shall be concerned in the next two chapters, we must consider them in some detail.

Now Clarke attempted to analyse the rightness of actions by expressly treating it as synonymous with their fittingness or suitability, and by asserting that this fittingness is derived from congruities and agreements in nature similar to those which in mathematics obtain between figures or numbers. The greater part of this analysis is summarized in the following passage:

'That there are differences of things; and different relations, respects or proportions, of some things towards others; is as evident and undeniable, as that one magnitude or number, is greater, equal to, or smaller than another. That from these different relations to different things, there necessarily arises an agreement or disagreement of some things with others or a fitness or unfitness of the application of different things or different relations one to another; is likewise as plain, as that there is any such thing as proportion or disproportion in geometry and arithmetic, or uniformity and difformity in comparing together the qualities and figures of bodies. Further, that there is a fitness or suitableness of certain circumstances to certain persons, and an unsuitableness of others; founded in the nature of things, and the qualifications of persons; antecedent to all positive appointment whatsoever; also, that from different relations of different persons one to another, there necessarily arises a fitness or unfitness of certain manners of behaviour of some persons towards others; is as manifest, as that the properties which flow from the essences of different mathematical figures, have different congruities or incongruities between themselves. . . .'[1]

[1] *A Discourse Concerning the Unchangeable Obligations of Natural Religion*, p. 46.

We can perhaps express this view more simply in the following way: There are differences in nature between things; some things are unlike others, as, for example, a circle is unlike a square. From these differences we can deduce that certain things agree with others in some respects and disagree in others, as a circle agrees with a square in being an extended two-dimensional figure and disagrees in having a round shape and not a square one. And further, Clarke argues, it follows from these agreements and disagreements that the 'application' of some things to others is fitting while to others it is not; as for instance it follows from the disagreement of squares and circles in respect of shape that round pegs are unfittingly applied to square holes and are fittingly applied to round ones. In precisely the same way we can speak of the fittingness and unfittingness of human actions to the circumstances in which they occur and to the people affected by them. Thus an act of keeping faith is fittingly applied to a situation in which a promise has been made, for there is a natural agreement between this act and the situation.[1] '. . . in men's dealings and conversings with one another; it is undeniably more fit, absolutely and in the nature of the thing itself, that all men should endeavour to promote the universal good and welfare of all; than that all men should be continually contriving the ruin and destruction of all.'[2]

Such is Clarke's endeavour to explain the attribution of rightness or fittingness to acts of well-doing, keeping faith, or preserving life—a rightness which they possess independently of the interest or feelings of the agent, of custom, and of con-

---

[1] Compare John Balguy, *The Foundation of Moral Goodness*, 1728, p. 36: 'To treat men in the same way we treat brutes, and to treat brutes in the same way we do stocks and stones, is manifestly as disagreeable and dissonant to the natures of things, as it would be to attempt the forming of an angle with two parallel lines.'

[2] *Obligations of Natural Religion*, p. 49. This passage continues as follows: 'It is evidently more fit, even before all positive bargains and compacts, that men should deal one with another according to the known rules of justice and equity; than that every man for his own present advantage, should without scruple disappoint the most reasonable and equitable expectations of his neighbours, and cheat and defraud, or spoil by violence, all others without restraint.'

vention. To show that propositions asserting that acts have this characteristic are capable of demonstration was, he thought, the main task of moral philosophy.

But although we can say that Clarke thought moral propositions were *primarily* concerned with rightness, he certainly thought they were also concerned with obligation—though the meaning he attaches to obligation is so vague that he often confuses the two. If his great virtue lies in his attempts to clarify rightness, his great failing rests in his indiscriminate use of 'obligation', a term of which he never offers any definition. We cannot say that he identifies 'right' with 'obligatory'. There is an obvious difference between rightness in Clarke's sense of the term, which is a characteristic an act possesses when it occurs, or would possess if it occurred, and obligation which, even as it is used by him, pertains to the act's occurrence. To say that an act is fitting and to say that fitting acts ought to be done is not the same, yet this is a distinction which Clarke to a large extent obscures.[1] He argues that 'it is fit that men should deal with one another according to the known laws of justice and equity', and in saying this he seems to imply not merely that acts of equity would be fitting if they occurred, but also that *ipso facto* they ought to be done. That this is his meaning is borne out by the passage where he argues that '. . . the mind of man cannot avoid giving its assent to the eternal law of Righteousness; that is cannot but acknowledge the reasonableness and fitness of men's governing all their actions by the rule of right or equity; and also that this assent is a formal obligation upon every man, actually and constantly to conform himself to that rule'.[2] Yet Clarke does not always fall into this confusion: sometimes he recognizes that it is one thing for an act to be fitting and quite another for it to be obligatory, for he says the will of man ought to be determined in every action by the 'reason of the thing' and the 'right of the case'. But, as we shall see, the problems raised by the recognition of this difference he avoids by main-

---

[1] See W. D. Falk, 'Obligation and Rightness', *Philosophy*, 1945.
[2] *Obligations of Natural Religion*, p. 81.

taining that it is self-contradictory to will acts which are known to be unfitting.[1]

Turning now from those philosophers who considered that moral propositions are mainly about rightness and fittingness to those who thought that they are primarily concerned with obligation, we find that the latter criticize Clarke on two grounds. First, they argue that his use of 'rightness' and 'fittingness' is unanalysed and meaningless in spite of his attempted precision; and secondly they maintain that to show that acts are right and fitting would not in any case, *ipso facto*, be to show that they are obligatory; and they imply that it is only when we show that an act is obligatory that a moral judgement is made.

It is not surprising that Clarke's attempted analysis of rightness should have provoked stern criticism; it is surprising that such criticism was only forthcoming some twenty years after the delivery of the Boyle Lectures in 1705. His analysis as it stands is very obscure. It is by no means as obvious as he thought that 'relations, respects and proportions between things' have a 'consequent agreement and disagreement', 'fitness and unfitness', and as to the manner in which he supposed them to have such a fitness and agreement he gives no indication. As John Clarke of Hull points out, 'The agreement of ideas is a phrase borrowed from Mr. Locke, in whose manner of using it, it is clear and intelligible'.[2] In Locke's view ideas can agree in respect of identity, relation, coexistence, and necessary connexion. In fact Locke uses 'agreement' as a generic term in much the same way that Hume uses 'resemblance'; he uses it to signify simply that two ideas possess some common characteristic. It seems possible that Clarke also used

---

[1] For similar views see John Clarke, Samuel's brother, Boyle Lectures delivered in 1719; Thomas Chubb, 'A Vindication of God's Moral Character', in a *Collection of Tracts* by him, 1730; Richard Fiddes, *Treatise of Morality*, 1724; and John Balguy, *Letter to a Deist Concerning the Beauty and Excellence of Moral Virtue*, 1726, and his *Foundation of Moral Goodness*, Part I, 1728, Part II, 1729. Also many second-rate philosophers.

[2] John Clarke, *An Examination of what has been Advanced relating to Moral Obligation in a late Pamphlet, entitled, A defence of an answer to remarks upon Dr. Clarke's exposition of the Church Catechism*, 1730, p. 14.

'agreement' in this way, but, as John Clarke points out, the only mode of agreement which is at all applicable to the examples of agreeing things Clarke cites is relation, and, as he concludes, if this was his meaning 'our author has strangely overseen, very short, I think, to leave things so much in the dark, by not specifying that relation, that we might judge for ourselves, how the perception of this relation, can make gratitude a moral duty, or lay an obligation upon men to the constant practice thereof. . . .'[1] If we reconsider our previous example of agreeing things, round pegs and round holes, it is clear that these can be said to agree in respect of shape, and perhaps also of size, i.e. the relations in which they agree are essentially spatial; but there does not seem to be any recognized philosophical relation in respect of which acts can be said to agree with situations, nor does Clarke attempt to show what this relation is.

Clarke's conception of *fittingness* is no less obscure than that of *agreement*. The fittingness of things, he argues, is derived from their agreement, yet fittingness, he thinks, is an absolute characteristic; it is 'absolute and in the nature of the thing itself'. But it certainly seems that if 'fittingness' is to mean anything at all it cannot signify any absolute quality, or even a relation in which *two* things stand to one another. In order to speak sensibly in saying that two things fit, we must specify some respect in which they fit. Things are not merely fitting to other things in themselves, but fitting to them in respect of something third: i.e. things are not merely fitting *to*, but also fitting *for*. Thus, for example, two pieces of a jigsaw puzzle

---

[1] Op. cit., p. 15. John Clarke continues as follows: 'For my part, I can think of no relation attached to those ideas, no relation of gratitude to kindness, but that of an effect to its cause, which yet belongs not to the ideas considered by themselves, (since there is no universal inseparable connection of that kind between gratitude and kindness received) but only in conjunction with the idea of a certain disposition of mind in the person who receives the kindness, necessary in order to its making that impression, or having that effect upon him; that is, in plain English, we find gratitude to be the natural product of kindness received, in minds, whose natural relish has not been vitiated by an indulgence of ill-natured passions. . . . The argument stands thus. Gratitude is generally the effect of kindness received, therefore it is a moral duty. And lewdness, say I, is generally the effect of keeping lewd company, therefore that is a moral duty too.'

fit each other in respect of shape for the purpose of completing a spatial whole; but these same two pieces may be unfitting in respect of the pictures on their surface, that is, for the purpose of completing a pictorial whole. If we are to agree with Clarke in saying that acts can fit the circumstances in which they occur, we must be able to specify in respect of what, and for what purpose, they are fitting. John Clarke and Francis Hutcheson both criticize Clarke on the grounds that he uses fittingness, an essentially relative term, in a non-relational sense. They both think that fittingness is a relation which holds, not between two things, but between three. Acts, they argue, can only fit situations if the ends of the agents, or of those affected by them, are taken into account. Thus John Clarke comments: 'I ask, therefore, when the practice of gratitude is said to be fit, for what is it fit?' It might be argued that Clarke recognized that fittingness was a relation of this kind, i.e. that he intended to argue that acts agree with situations in respect of the fulfilling of the ends of those affected by them, and are fittingly applied for this purpose. But had he admitted this, he would have been faced with questions he could not well have answered, for once it is assumed that the fittingness of actions holds between acts and ends in respect of the latter's fulfilment, it is evident that the fittingness of acts is strictly relative to the ends for which they are fit, and must vary concomitantly with them. As Hutcheson observes, if we call the suitability of acts for the achievement of ends fit

'. . . then the most contrary actions have equal fitnesses for contrary ends; and each one is unfit for the end of the other. Thus compassion is fit to make others happy, and unfit to make them miserable. Violation of property is fit to make men miserable, and unfit to make them happy. Each of these is both fit and unfit, with respect to different ends.'[1]

He concludes that, since there is no absolute but only relative fitness, fitness cannot be the proper subject of moral proposi-

[1] *Nature and Conduct of the Passions and Affections*, p. 249. See also John Clarke, *Foundations of Morality*, p. 32, where he describes the fittingness of the application of hemlock and ratsbane to the human body 'to the production of sickness and pain, and thereby to the destruction of life'.

tions; the bare fitness to an end is not the idea of moral goodness. For an act is fitting only for given ends, and if such ends
are arbitrarily selected, then not all actions can be *morally*
fitting; or acts are morally fitting because they are means to
some ultimate end, and then their morality does not depend
upon their fittingness but upon this end, for, as Hutcheson
writes, 'an ultimate end' is 'not fit for anything further'.[1]

Such was the criticism raised against the Clarkians' termino-
logy; but John Clarke and Hutcheson had also a more fundamental criticism to offer. In their view, Clarke was wrong in
thinking that the main task of moral philosophy is to show how
propositions about rightness are meaningful and capable of
rational verification. Moral propositions, they thought, are
concerned not with *rightness* but with *obligation*, and they
argued that to show of acts that if they occurred they would
stand in a relation of fittingness to the situation, i.e. be right,
is not to show that agents are obliged to do acts of this kind.
This argument is of general interest. It must be met, not only
by those who think that the morality of acts consists in their
rightness or fittingness, but by anyone who maintains that for
an act to be 'moral' is for it to be such as would possess some
characteristic when or if it occurred. Whether this characteristic is goodness, or fittingness, or the promotion of the
happiness of the agent is irrelevant. It must be met by Mill as
by Clarke, and to-day by Professor Moore as by Sir David
Ross.

Now it is true, as we have seen, that Clarke does not always
identify propositions about fittingness with those about obligation. At times he tries to show that right or fitting acts are
also obligatory: indicating that he was aware of a distinction
between the meaning of these two terms. Nor do his critics
expressly attack him for the view that fittingness is the object
of moral statements; but they do maintain that all his arguments about fittingness and rightness, even if they had independent validity, would leave unsolved the problem of
obligation. For merely to think of an act as being of a certain

[1] *Of the Passions*, p. 250.

kind, as being fitting, or being an act of bounty or gratitude, is not *ipso facto* to think of an obligation to do it. This point could not have been made more clearly than by Balguy's anonymous correspondent, possibly Hutcheson, who wrote:

'The ideas of bounty and gratitude are, if you please, moral ideas; but no moral propositions can rightly be deduced from them: or however, no such proposition as includes any sort of obligation. From the mere idea of gratitude, it will no more follow that men ought to be grateful, than from the idea of ingratitude, that they ought to be ungrateful, if we suppose no sentiment.' 'If we had otherwise no idea of obligation, the ideas of gratitude, ingratitude and bounty, could never so much as afford us a general idea of obligation itself; or inform us what is meant by that term; much less could we be able to deduce the particular obligation to gratitude from these ideas.'[1]

This argument is plain. Being obligatory is not like being bountiful or being fitting, a characteristic which an act would possess if and when it occurred. From this it follows that we cannot by simply examining such a characteristic discover anything about the act being or not being obligatory. The force of this argument was, however, considerably lessened by the fact that those who advanced it themselves omitted to say precisely what they meant by obligation. Very definite views about it are certainly implicit in their arguments. Being obliged was, they thought, a 'state of mind' of an agent, a state of feeling prompted to do some action by the thought of it; and on this view of obligation it is clear that no act can rightly be called obligatory unless it can be shown that the agent has a motive or impelling reason for doing it. The arguments of the anti-Clarkian school all rested on this view of obligation, and they would have acquired great additional force if these philosophers had advanced and defended a precise definition. In fact they say no more than that to have an obligation is to have an 'exciting reason' for doing an action, while they fail to discuss properly what kind of exciting reason this is. Hutche-

[1] John Balguy, *The Second Part of The Foundation of Moral Goodness*, 1729, Articles 3 and 4. In this tract Balguy defends himself against a critic of the first part which was itself largely directed against Hutcheson. The criticisms are quoted as articles which Balguy answers in turn.

son seems to identify being obliged with being impelled by the thought of the well-being of others, though he is most clear that to promote their well-being cannot be a duty unless we are impelled by the thought of it:

'If any allege as the reason exciting us to pursue the public good, this truth, that "the happiness of a system, a thousand or a million, is a greater quantity of happiness than that of one person: and consequently, if men desire happiness, they must have stronger desires toward the greater sum, than toward the less." This reason still supposes an instinct toward happiness as previous to it: . . . without such [public] affections this truth, "that an hundred felicities is a greater sum than one felicity", will no more excite to study the happiness of the hundred, than this truth, "an hundred stones are greater than one", will excite a man, who has no desire of heaps, to cast them together.'[1]

John Clarke seems to have identified the exciting reason for doing moral acts with the agent's conception of his own happiness. He was in fact a hedonist. His argument in this respect is a mere appendage to Hutcheson's: it is by no means necessary to maintain that we are moved only by the thought of pleasure— a dubious assertion—in order to argue either that to be obliged we must be moved, or that fitting actions cannot be obligations unless we are moved by the thought of them. Yet John Clarke puts forward his argument with so much vigour, and compared with Clarke's dry academics it savours so wholesome, that I cannot forbear quoting the most forceful passage at length:

'Relations, respects, differences, fitness and unfitness in things themselves, whatever those words signify, when separated from all consideration or expectation of pleasure or pain, happiness or misery, are but empty sounds, no proper basis or support for morality at all; and which, when brought to trial, will no more be able to stand it against pleasure and pain, than dust before a whirlewind, or stubble before the devouring flames. The considerations of pleasure and pain, present or future, will and must operate upon the mind, in spite of all the empty airy motives from bare relations, respects, etc. And to expect the mind should be influenced by consideration of differences, relations, fitness, unfitness, etc. in opposition to that prodigious impulse given it, by the

[1] *Of the Passions*, p. 222.

considerations of happiness or misery, is much the same as to think of battering down mighty walls, by the puffing feathers against them.'[1]

It would not be fair to Clarke to say that he was altogether unaware of the difficulties which these arguments raised. To some extent he recognized that fittingness and obligation are distinct, and that there is difficulty in saying we are obliged to do fitting acts without indicating any motives for our doing them. 'The practice of vice,' he remarks, 'that is the doing of unfitting acts, is accompanied by great temptations and allurements of pleasure and profit, and the practice of virtue is often threatened with great calamities, losses and sometimes even with death itself.'[2] Therefore only a few can be virtuous in such circumstances. 'Men never will generally, and indeed it is not very reasonably to be expected they should, part with all the comforts of life, and even life itself; without expectation of any future recompense.'[3] Clarke, however, is unwilling to argue that the knowledge of future recompense is what actually makes an act obligatory, though without it he thinks we could not do obligatory acts:

'. . . if we suppose no future state of reward, it will follow that God has endued men with such faculties, as put them under that necessity of approving and choosing virtue . . . and yet has not given them where-with to support themselves in the suitable and constant practice of it.'[3]

The question of whether we could be obliged or not without rewards and punishments is left open, for Clarke would be unwilling to admit either that we can be obliged to do those acts which we cannot do, or that our obligations can depend on the motive of expected reward. It is evident that if he had adopted the latter alternative the necessary condition of obligation would have been transferred from the fittingness of the acts to the expectation of reward, and were the divine system of allotting rewards and punishments changed so that fitting acts were punished and unfitting rewarded, unfitting acts would become obligations. Clarke did not in fact place the essence

[1] *Foundations of Morality*, p. 8.
[2] *Obligations of Natural Religion*, p. 117.
[3] Ibid., p. 119.

of morality in expectation of rewards and punishments, yet, in so far as he did not do this, the introduction of these external sanctions had little value; for if he wished to maintain that men are obliged independently of sanctions, then he would have had to show how they can be obliged without them.

Here, it is interesting to note that, in spite of the uselessness of introducing sanctions to bolster up a moral law which is not compelling by itself, Clarke, in so doing, was in good company. The precedent had been set by most seventeenth-century moralists, very notably by Malebranche. They failed to notice that either acts are obligatory without sanctions, and then the introduction of them is superfluous since it cannot make them more obligatory; or they are not obligatory without them, in which case the respect for external sanctions becomes part of the essence of morality, and all their arguments placing the obligatoriness of acts in their reasonableness or fittingness can be dispensed with. Spinoza was almost alone in recognizing this fact:

'. . . we may, with reason,' he writes, 'regard as a great absurdity what many, who are otherwise esteemed as great theologians, assert, namely, that if no eternal life resulted from the love of God, then they would seek what is best for themselves: as though they could discover anything better than God! This is just as silly as if a fish (for which, of course, it is impossible to live out of the water) were to say: if no eternal life is to follow this life in the water, then I will leave the water for the land. . . .'[1]

Having pursued the early eighteenth-century views of the proper subject of moral propositions to this point, we must now turn to the conceptions that were current of their rational proof. Here too we find that the suggestions of the seventeenth century reappear in an elaborated form. Though the view that moral propositions are self-evident because they agree with innate ideas has disappeared, they are still regarded as self-evident on the ground that *a priori* reasoning can show that the omission of some acts and doing of others is itself contrary to reason. In the seventeenth century, as we have seen, this

---

[1] *God, Man and his Well-being*, translation by A. Wolf, 1910, p. 145.

view never occurs by itself; in the eighteenth, on the other hand, it always occurs in isolation from its empirical alternative. As might be expected, the group of philosophers who accept this view is composed mainly of Clarke and his followers, though it also contains Wollaston.

Clarke's own theory seems to have been a conjunction of Malebranche's somewhat vague utterances about the 'nature and reason of things' and Hobbes's remark that 'injustice is absurdity in conversation'—a statement which Clarke reformulates as 'iniquity is the very same in action as contradiction in theory'. In Hobbes this was only a passing remark; in Malebranche the 'reason of things' played a considerable part, but what he meant by it remained exceedingly obscure and general. Clarke, on the other hand, advances 'iniquity is contradiction' as an elaborate theory. He seems to have arrived at this theory by two separate stages, which were in a large degree confused. First he maintained that judgements about fittingness were *a priori*—in asserting that some acts are fitting and others unfitting we assert what is self-evident or self-contradictory; secondly, he argued that in doing unfitting acts and in omitting to do fitting ones men behave in a self-contradictory manner. These two arguments are in fact distinct, and although Clarke confuses them, and it is never wholly clear to which he is referring when he speaks of morals as demonstrable, we must review them separately.

Let us begin by considering the arguments for the demonstrability of propositions about fittingness. According to Clarke, 'For a man endued with reason, to deny the truth of these things is the very same thing, as if a man . . . that understands geometry or arithmetic, should . . . perversely contend that the whole is not equal to all its parts, or that a square is not double to a triangle of equal base and height.'[1] It seems that Clarke was only enabled to make this dogmatic and very questionable statement because he failed to analyse fittingness in sufficient detail. Whether or not propositions about fittingness are demonstrable depends on the terms between which

[1] *Unchangeable Obligations*, p. 50.

the relation is supposed to hold. The proposition: 'round pegs are fittingly applied to round holes of an appropriate size for the purpose of completing a spatial whole' is evidently *a priori*. But whether it is altogether fitting to apply pegs to holes in this manner depends also on whether it is anyone's end to complete spatial wholes in this way. That anyone has or has not this end is an empirical fact. Moreover, whether any given peg is fittingly applied to any given hole depends on whether these pegs and holes are in fact perfectly round and of an appropriate size, which again are empirical conditions. Hence the proposition 'it is fitting to put this peg into this hole because both are round' is empirical even if one of its premisses is *a priori*.

In all fairness to Clarke we must allow that when he speaks of *a priori* fittingness it is mainly such fittingness that he has in mind. Many of his examples, however, are of quite a different kind. The assertion that acts of gratitude are fitting is in no degree *a priori*, for it does not even rest on an *a priori* premiss about what ends acts of gratitude are fitting to. It is not demonstrably certain that an act of gratitude if joined to the expectations of a sentient being must be conducive to his ends.

It may perhaps be objected to this argument that, when Clarke asserts that we can know *a priori* that gratitude is fitting whereas ingratitude is not, he is not referring to a fittingness of grateful acts to the ends of sentient beings for the purpose of their realization, but either to their fittingness to something else or to some unspecified fittingness in general. But, if this is so, then in order to maintain that propositions about fittingness are *a priori* he would have to show either that there is something other than ends to which acts can be fitting, or else that acts can be intrinsically fitting without being fitting to anything in particular. But in fact he does not attempt to show that either of these alternatives is the case, and indeed there is good reason to suppose that any such attempt would be doomed to failure.

Now we said that Clarke wished to maintain that we can

know *a priori* not merely that certain acts are fitting but also that fitting acts ought to be done. We know *a priori* that fitting acts are duties, because to deny that they are duties is to assert a self-contradiction: the *doing* of unfitting acts and the *not doing* of fitting ones is itself contrary to the laws of logic.

'So far', Clarke writes, 'as men are conscious of what is right and wrong, so far they are under an obligation to act accordingly: and consequently that eternal rule of right . . . ought as indispensably to govern men's actions, as it cannot but necessarily determine their assent.'[1]

and again:

'All wilful wickedness and perversion of right, is the very same insolence and absurdity in moral matters, as it would be in natural things, for a man to pretend to alter certain proportions of numbers, to take away the demonstrable relation, and properties of mathematical figures, to make light darkness and darkness light.'[2]

and again:

'Iniquity is the very same in action, as falsity or contradiction in theory.'[3]

Here Clarke is using 'contradictory' and 'absurd' in a very peculiar way. Actions, he argues, can be absurd, and he repeatedly compares their absurdity to that of false mathematical judgements. There is the same absurdity in acting contrary to justice as there is in the assertion that twice two is not equal to four. But clearly, as we shall see Hume points out, *acts* cannot be absurd or self-contradictory; absurdity and contradiction belong to *propositions* and not to real existents. In defence of Clarke it may perhaps be argued that in calling acts absurd he did not intend to be taken literally. What he meant

---

[1] *Unchangeable Obligations*, p. 70.    [2] Ibid., p. 167.
[3] Ibid., p. 86. See also p. 65, where Clarke writes: '. . . it is as natural and (morally speaking) necessary, that the will should be determined in every action by the reason of the thing and the right of the case; as it is natural and (absolutely speaking) necessary, that the understanding should submit to a demonstrated truth . . . it is as absurd and blame-worthy, to mistake negligently plain right and wrong, that is, to understand the proportions of things in morality to be what they are not; or wilfully to act contrary to known justice and equity, that is, to will things to be what they are not and cannot be; as it would be absurd and ridiculous for a man in arithmetical matters, ignorantly to believe that twice two is not equal to four.'

to convey was merely that some acts are logically impossible, i.e. that there are some acts of which we cannot say that they occur without contradicting ourselves.

But, even if this is what Clarke intended to say, he has still to show that unfitting acts or rather the willing of unfitting acts is logically impossible, i.e. that the assertion '$x$ wills an unfitting act $y$' is self-contradictory; and even if the arguments by which he tries to show that the fittingness of acts can be known *a priori* were valid, they would have been of no avail here. For the logical impossibility of making a given act fitting to a given situation does not entail the logical impossibility of willing unfitting acts. All that Clarke could have maintained was that it is logically impossible to will to combine two things fittingly of which we know that they cannot be so combined; e.g. to will to fit round pegs into square holes if we know this to be logically impossible, or to will to make ingratitude fit with the expectations of a benefactor if we know that this combination is unfitting. But there is no logical impossibility in willing unfitting combinations: to bring round pegs and square holes together in a way in which they do not fit each other, or to join ingratitude to the expectations of a benefactor in a way which leaves our action unfitting to the situation in which it occurs.

It seems that Clarke was led to adopt this view by a curious oversight. We have already noticed that, in arguing that moral propositions can be known to be true *a priori*, he in fact maintains two things: first, that we know *a priori* what acts are fitting, and secondly, that we know *a priori* that fitting acts ought to be done. It seems as though he began by thinking that the assertion that certain acts are fitting was self-contradictory, but that from this by a simple transfer of epithet he arrived at the conclusion that the acts themselves are self-contradictory. It seems possible that this occurred as follows: (i) He argued that it was unreasonable to assert that unfitting acts are fitting; (ii) he began to call such acts unreasonable by way of abbreviation; (iii) he forgot that the word 'unreasonable' applied to the proposition and not to the act itself; (iv) he began to apply it to the act when he was thinking of its occurrence and not its unfittingness; (v) he concluded that it was unreasonable to do unfitting acts. Such a procedure is of course totally illegitimate, but it saved Clarke from the difficulties he would have met in answering the all-important question: Why are fitting acts obligatory?—a question which those who hold his views about morality and fittingness always find difficult to answer. It is highly significant, however, that he escaped this predicament because he transferred the word 'reasonable' to the act itself from that very proposition which asserted that the act was fitting. His argument amounted to saying: 'It is unreasonable to say that unjust acts are fitting, therefore it is unreasonable to do unjust acts.' It would have had just as much and just as little validity, though it would have been quite worthless for the purpose of side-tracking the question of why fitting acts are obligatory, if he had said: 'It is unreasonable to assert that unjust acts are green, therefore it is unreasonable to do unjust acts.' It was against the arguments that the morality of acts is dependent upon the truth of propositions about them that Hutcheson argued: 'If conformity to truth or reasonableness denote nothing else but that "an action is the object of a true proposition", 'tis plain that all actions should be approved equally, since as many truths may be made about the worst, as can be made about the best.'[1] '. . . any man may make as many truths about villainy, as about heroism, by ascribing to it contrary attributes.'[2]

Clarke and his school were not the only philosophers who thought moral propositions capable of demonstration. There was also Wollaston. Wollaston accepted Clarke's statement that 'iniquity is the very same in action as contradiction in theory' at its face value. His whole philosophy is in fact an elaboration of this view. When he asserts that acts are absurd he is to be taken literally; he does not mean that in willing such acts we are willing the impossible, but literally that we are contradicting ourselves. Unlike Clarke, Wollaston was aware

[1] *Of the Passions*, p. 226.          [2] Ibid., p. 214.

that self-contradiction can only be attributed to assertions, but he tried to avoid this difficulty by holding the strange view that all acts are assertions. When I steal a horse I assert that the horse is mine; when I live beyond my means I assert that I have more money than I in fact possess; when I refuse to give alms to a beggar I deny that he is in need. All acts assert propositions, and when an act asserts a false proposition—whether its falsity is *a priori* or empirical is irrelevant —in asserting it I am contradicting myself. I am asserting both *a* and not-*a* at the same time; I am in fact making two contradictory assertions. Moreover, I am 'willing things to be what they are not and cannot be'.

Thus Wollaston adopts Clarke's theory that those acts are obligatory of which it can be shown that they are intrinsically reasonable. But he differs from Clarke in that he dispenses altogether with the latter's analysis of rightness as fittingness. In fact he does not attribute the morality of acts to any characteristic which they would have if they occurred, but simply to their logical self-consistency. In so far as he uses the word 'right' he uses it as synonymous with 'true', in the sense in which we say 'That's right', meaning 'That's the case'. He is of course only able to apply 'right' in this sense to acts because he holds the very odd theory that acts can be true: 'If that proposition, which is false, be wrong, that act which *implies* such a proposition, or is founded in it cannot be right; because it is the very proposition itself in practice.'[1]

Yet Wollaston's position is beset with difficulties. Even if we were to admit that acts assert propositions, we would still be at a loss to know why those which assert false propositions are self-contradictory. Evidently Wollaston thinks that when I steal a horse I know that the horse is not mine and my act in stealing it contradicts this knowledge. But even though my act in stealing it really were to assert that the horse was mine, it would still only be contradictory to my *knowledge* and not to another *assertion*, for I would not have asserted that the horse belonged to somebody else. This clearly is the case with all

---

[1] *Religion of Nature Delineated*, 1724, p. 13.

intentionally false statements; lies express what the speaker believes to be untrue, but they do not at the same time give expression to this belief. Moreover, even if we were to admit that when a man steals a horse he is asserting both that it is his and that it is not his at the same time, then though we would indeed have to allow that he was asserting a contradiction, yet it would only be *what he asserted* and not the *act of asserting* which could properly be called self-contradictory. Plainly it is possible to say 'black cats are not black' and the act of saying this does not contradict itself. Thus even if Wollaston had succeeded in showing that all acts are symbolic, he would not have shown that they are what he called 'propositions in practice'. For all propositions, even those that are stated verbally, are different from the acts of stating them; it is never the act of stating but only what is stated which can be in conformity with, or contrary to, the laws of logic. Hence Wollaston's recognition that only assertions can be self-contradictory, and his consequent attempt to show that acts do assert something was of no avail. For he confused 'asserting' with 'assertion', and although he said that acts are propositions he did not even try to show that acts are actually assertions but only that they are acts of asserting.

In any event the argument that all acts assert propositions is a fantastic one, and it was made even odder by Wollaston's contention that the criterion by which we discover what it is that an act asserts is not the intention of the agent but the conclusions which the spectator draws from it. It is not what I intend people to understand by my riding of a stolen horse which constitutes its meaning, but the inferences which they in fact draw.

Clarke, as we have seen, held what amounted to an essentially negative view of moral action. Actions, he argued, ought to be done when their omission is self-contradictory. Wollaston, on the other hand, took the positive view that men are obliged not merely to avoid what is self-contradictory but to do what is self-consistent: not merely to avoid falsehood but to assert truth. No doubt he thought that refraining from asserting true

propositions, equally with asserting false ones, was to behave
in a self-contradictory way, but he is not clear on this point.
It is interesting to note that John Clarke and Hutcheson—in
spite of all the latter's polite remarks about the ill-naturedness
of writing a censure 'of a book so well designed as Mr. Wollaston's, and so full of very good reasoning upon the most
useful subjects'— pointed out the odd implications of this view.
'Is it virtue to say at Christmas that the mornings are sharp?'[1]
wrote Hutcheson, and John Clarke '. . . it will then be a glorious
exercise for a man to spend his time thrumming over such
worthy and weighty propositions as these, "a man's no horse,
a horse no cow, a cow no bull, nor a bull an ass" '.[2]

Queer-headed though Wollaston was, he seems to have been
less inclined than Clarke to overlook the difficulties of his views.
He had a certain fundamental honesty suitable to one of his
opinions. Since the morality of actions depends on the truth
and falsehood of what they assert, and since nothing can be
more or less true or false, it follows from Wollaston's view that
all acts must be equally moral or immoral, a difficulty which
confronted Clarke also, for nothing can be more or less self-
contradictory, but which he ignored. Wollaston thought of an
ingenious solution. To steal a thousand pounds was, he said,
a thousand times worse than to steal one pound, because in
doing so we are contradicting a thousand true propositions,
and doing a thousand self-contradictory acts.[3]  But here a new
difficulty is introduced, for if one act can assert several pro-

---

[1] *Of the Passions*, p. 261.

[2] *Examination of the Notion of Good and Evil, advanced in a late book entitled
the Religion of Nature Delineated*, 1725, p. 19; see also p. 49. '. . . As if God
were more concerned to have things owned for what they are, than to see his
creatures contribute mutually to one another's happiness, which is representing
him as an odd kind of capricious being (with reverence be it spoken) whose
satisfaction consists in something, for which it is impossible the rational part
of creation should have any real reverence or veneration for him.'

[3] *Religion of Nature Delineated*, p. 21: 'If A steals a book from B which was
pleasing and useful to him, it is true A is guilty of a crime in not treating the
book as being what it is, the book of B, . . . but still if A should deprive B of
a good estate . . . he would be guilty of a much greater crime. For if we suppose
the book to be worth to him one pound, and the estate 10000 l. that truth, which
is violated by depriving B of his book, is in effect violated 10000 times by robbing
him of his estate.'

positions, some may be false and others true, and Wollaston does not seem to have been satisfied with counting the number of truths asserted, subtracting the falsehoods, and saying that that act which asserts most truths is the most moral. He introduces instead a criterion for estimating the *value* of the truths asserted: the most 'important' truths are those which contribute most to the happiness of mankind.[1] With this his rationalist analysis breaks down; the whole edifice of truths and falsehoods becomes a clumsy superstructure to the relatively simple view that moral acts are those which we judge to be conducive to the happiness of mankind.

Wollaston like Clarke was criticized by both John Clarke and Hutcheson. Both question his fundamental assumption that acts are assertions. '. . . affirming and denying', writes John Clarke, 'are actions which in a strict propriety of language are only applicable to agents; so that actions, whether words or deeds, can not be properly said to affirm or deny any thing; the agent only can be properly said to affirm or deny truth by his actions. . . .'[2] Hence, he argues, acts cannot be said to have meaning unless the agent intends to convey knowledge by them, and the great majority of acts, both moral and immoral, are not of this kind.

Hutcheson criticized Wollaston's main contention, namely that immoral acts are those whereby the agent asserts two contradictory propositions:

'. . . 'tis to be doubted', he wrote, 'that such madness ever happened to even the worst of mankind. When a man murders, he does not desire his fellow creature to be both dead and living. When he robs, he does not desire that both he and the proprietor should at the same time possess.'[3]

---

[1] In spite of this admission Wollaston argued that acts which 'interfere with the nature and truth and deny the nature of things' cannot promote happiness. The position was further confused by his reversal of this into 'those maxims may be esteemed the natural and true laws of any particular society, which are most proper to procure the happiness of it' (p. 128).

[2] *Examination of the Notion of Moral Good and Evil*, p. 6. Thus John Clarke recognized that acts do not assert propositions, but overlooked Wollaston's further error in asserting that an act by which an agent asserts a proposition and the proposition which he asserts are the same.

[3] *Of the Passions*, p. 272.

And John Clarke comments somewhat more maliciously:

'. . . who besides himself could have found out, for instance, that to commit fornication, is to deny that there is so much as one woman in the world; and to get drunk, is to deny that there is one drop of liquor, strong or small, for a man to quench his thirst with, upon the face of the whole earth.'[1]

Thus the view that moral action is logically consistent action, immoral self-contradictory, fell into a state of disrepute when its most consistent exposition came into the hands of John Clarke and Hutcheson. Yet its disrepute did not extend beyond philosophers, and not even to all of them, for by many it was still accepted with great enthusiasm, and *The Religion of Nature Delineated* had a far larger sale than the *Treatise*. Moreover, Hume evidently considered that this view stood in need of further criticism, for, as we shall see, he paid considerable attention to it.

Such were the arguments of those early eighteenth-century moralists who tried to show that reason can verify moral propositions *a priori*. The eighteenth-century empiricists we need only consider briefly, for we have already noted most of their arguments in reviewing their criticism of their *a priori* opponents.

Among those who in practice rejected the Clarke–Wollaston conception of rational verification was Bishop Butler. He was the first to distinguish explicitly between *a priori* and empirical methods, and although he paid lip service to the former he made his preference for the latter perfectly clear, and it was this latter method which he himself adopted. In the Preface to the *Sermons* we find the following passage:

'There are two ways in which the subject of morals may be treated. One begins from enquiring into the abstract relations of things: the other from a matter of fact, namely, what the particular nature of man is, its several parts, their economy or constitution; from whence it proceeds to determine what course of life it is, which is correspondent to this whole nature. In the former method the conclusion is expressed thus, that vice is contrary to the nature and reason of things: in the latter, that it is a violation or breaking in upon our own nature. Thus

[1] *Examination of Moral Good, etc.*, p. 45.

they both lead us to the same thing, our obligations to the practice of virtue; and thus they exceedingly strengthen and enforce each other. The first seems the most direct formal proof, and in some respects the least liable to cavil and dispute: the latter is in a peculiar manner adapted to satisfy a fair mind: and is more easily applicable to the several particular relations and circumstances in life.'[1]

We may say that by 1730 the *a priori* and empirical methods were strictly divided; and while Butler seems to have stood alone in arguing that both, though distinct, were equally applicable, in practice he too only applies the one. We can say, too, that the majority of reputable philosophers agreed in abandoning *a priori* arguments. Yet when we come to consider the positive views of Clarke's critics, we find that the empirical method too has its own confusions and difficulties.

Their main argument against Clarke was, as we have seen, that reason in verifying the kind of propositions with which Clarke was concerned discovers nothing which must affect the agent's will. From this it follows that if these philosophers are to be consistent and yet allow that reason can discover moral laws, they must argue that reason in doing so can discover a special motive to action. Hutcheson and Butler alone explicitly recognize this fact. John Clarke and others held the common view that moral propositions state no more than that certain acts are conducive to the lasting happiness of the agent.[2] It is true that John Clarke implies that the discovery that an act is an obligation must be the discovery that the agent is moved by the thought of it, but his arguments are all directed to show, not that the agent must be moved by the thought of those acts which are obligatory, but that the only ideas which he can be moved by are ideas of acts which contribute to his well-being.

[1] Butler, *Sermons*, Gladstone's edition, 1897, Preface, p. 5.
[2] See John Clarke, *The Foundations of Morality*, p. 25: 'The wise and the foolish, the virtuous and the vicious . . . stand distinguished only by this circumstance of their behaviour that the former, . . . examine into the nature of things, and their consequences, and waive their present interest . . . for the sake of greater to come; whilst the foolish and vicious are apt to rush inconsiderately and blindly forward, without any due regard to what may follow hereafter.' Compare passages quoted from Hobbes and Grotius above, p. 10. See also John Gay, in Selby-Bigge's *British Moralists*, p. 73, where he defines obligation as the necessity of doing or omitting any action in order to be happy.

Being morally obliged, he thought, differs from mere desiring in that we are obliged only when we are moved by the thought of acts which lead to lasting and not merely temporary happiness. This shift of emphasis from the necessity of showing that agents must be moved, to what it is by which they are moved, obscures the force of the empiricist argument.

Butler also intimated the essentially practical nature of moral reasoning. 'Man', he argues, 'is a law unto himself', and moral acts are those to which he is moved by feelings with authority. It is true that he draws no clear distinction between occasions on which we realize that actions are in accordance with our whole nature and others when we realize that we are authoritatively moved to do them; yet he makes it clear that the obligatoriness of an action is not a quality which it possesses independently of an agent, but a relation in which it stands to his conscience. 'The several passions and affections in the heart of man . . . lead him to a certain determinate course of action . . . they show us what course of life we are made for, what our duty is, and in a peculiar manner they enforce on us the practice of it.'[1]

Hutcheson is still more explicit on this point. Judgements about the obligatoriness of acts must provide the agent with 'exciting reasons' for doing them; and, since exciting reasons cannot exist independently of our desires, and since desires are empirical facts, it follows that *a priori* reasoning cannot verify moral propositions: 'As if indeed reason, or the knowledge of the relations of things, could excite to action when we proposed no end, or as if ends could be intended without desire or affection.'[2] Hutcheson was the first eighteenth-century philosopher to make this point in such indisputable terms, though it is true that in the seventeenth century Spinoza put forward similar arguments:

'The true knowledge of good and evil cannot exert any restraining influence on the affections in so far as it is true but only in so far as it is considered an affection.'[3]

[1] *Sermons*, p. 92.          [2] *Of the Passions*, p. 217.
[3] *Ethics*, Part IV, Proposition XIV.

But the significance of this argument was not fully realized. We have said that Hutcheson made it clear that judgements which verify moral propositions must also be capable of influencing us to action, but his analysis of these judgements remained obscure. Sometimes, in fact most frequently, he seems to argue that practical reasoning does no more than discover means to ends. Thus in his book *Of the Passions* he asks himself the question: '. . . are there no exciting reasons, even previous to any ends, moving us to propose one end rather than another?' and he replies:

'To this Aristotle long ago answered that "there are ultimate ends desired without a view to anything else, and subordinate ends or objects desired with a view to something else". To subordinate ends those reasons or truths excite, which show them to be conducive to the ultimate end, and show one object to be more effectual than another: thus subordinate ends may be called reasonable. But as to these ultimate ends, to suppose exciting reasons for them, would infer that there is no ultimate end, but that we desire one thing for another in an infinite series.'[1]

But Hutcheson, like Hume himself, at times maintains a far more liberal view of the influence of reason on action. Men, he argues, are influenced not merely by considering what ends certain actions lead to, but what qualities the ends themselves possess. There is, he thinks, a difference between accepting an end impulsively and accepting it after a thorough examination of the objects at which it aims:

'There is one general observation to be premised, which appears of the greatest necessity for the just management of all our desires; viz., that we should . . . prevent the violence of their confused sensation, and stop their propensities from breaking out into action, till we have fully examined the real moment of the object either of our desires or aversions. . . .'[2]

It seems to be to this function of reason he again refers when he writes:

'He acts reasonably, who considers the various actions in his power, and forms true opinions of their tendencies; and then chooses to do

---

[1] *Of the Passions*, p. 217.          [2] Ibid., p. 165.

that which will obtain the highest degree of that to which the instincts of his nature incline him.'[1]

The precise nature of Hutcheson's conception of the rational verification of moral propositions is complicated by his view that there are both moral and non-moral obligations. His analysis of the influence of reason on action is inadequate and his application of his conclusions to the problem of moral judgements is misleading. At times he even appears to dissociate reason from morality altogether and to deny that moral judgements are possible. His great merit consisted, not in showing *how* reason can verify practical propositions, but that reasoning, if it is to verify them, must be practical.

This then was the situation of moral philosophy at the time when Hume wrote the *Treatise*. Moralists of all schools believed that in one way or another morality depended on reason. But what this dependence implied was a matter of most far-reaching disagreement. Thus there was urgent need for a critical examination of the conflicting approaches to the problem. It was this need which Hume, in the second and third books of the *Treatise*, set out to satisfy.

[1] *Of the Passions*, p. 223. The relative parts played in the determination of action by reason and the passions is described in an anonymous book entitled *Virtue and Happiness*, 2nd edition, 1736; see p. 110: '... human life may in some respects, though imperfectly, be compared to a vessel at sea, where the winds which swell the sails, and put the vessel into motion, are the affections and passions; and reason is the master, who presides at the helm, and gives orders when to crowd, and when to furl the sails; when to go right before, and when to work against the wind ... if there were no wind stirring the ship would be perfectly becalmed and without motion; and when it blows a fresh gale, if there was no pilot to take care of the helm, but the vessel must be left to drive before the winds, she could never keep a steady course, nor reach the place for which she was bound, but would soon be dashed upon the rocks, or swallowed up by the merciless waves.'

# CHAPTER II

## FITTINGNESS AND OBLIGATION

WE have seen that the majority of moralists writing in the hundred and twenty years preceding the publication of the *Treatise* tried, in one way or another, to identify moral with rational action. Some went farther than others in understanding the implications of such an identification, but none succeeded in giving a precise description of the rational processes involved, or indeed in showing that such processes are possible. Hume set out to examine this problem anew. He observes that:

'Nothing is more usual in philosophy, and even in common life, than to talk of the combat of passion and reason, to give the preference to reason, and assert that men are only so far virtuous as they conform themselves to its dictates. Every rational creature, it is said, is obliged to regulate his actions by reason; and if any other motive or principle challenge the direction of his conduct, he ought to oppose it, till it be entirely subdued, or at least brought to a conformity with that superior principle.'[1]

But, Hume argues, if moral conduct rests on reason, this can only mean that it rests on judgement, for to reason is to judge, and further it must rest on either demonstrative or empirical judgement, for all judgements are of one of these two kinds. 'The understanding exerts itself after two different ways, as it judges from demonstration or probability, as it regards the abstract relations of our ideas, or those relations of objects of which experience only gives us information.'[2] It follows that anybody who wishes to maintain that moral conduct rests on reason must show that it rests on judgements of one of these two kinds: judgements about a relation of implication holding between ideas, or judgements about matters of fact.

Hume was concerned with the whole problem of rationalism in ethics, but he was above all interested in exposing the diffi-

---

[1] Hume, *Treatise of Human Nature*, Everyman, vol. ii, p. 125.
[2] Ibid.

culties of the widely accepted assumption that moral conduct is based on *a priori* judgements. The two prevailing types of the *a priori* view were those expounded by Clarke and by Wollaston. In this and the following chapter we shall be concerned with Hume's consideration and rejection of these two doctrines.

The philosopher who wishes to maintain that moral conduct rests on *a priori* judgements is, according to Hume, faced with two problems: he has to show, first, what the judgements on which moral conduct rests are about, and, secondly, how such judgements can be *a priori*. Hume's discussion of these two problems takes the form of a criticism of Samuel Clarke and his school. Clarke, as we have seen, supports his ·contention that moral judgements are *a priori* by two different arguments which he at times confuses. To act morally is to do right acts, right acts are fitting acts, and that some acts are fitting and others not can be known with certainty; here is one *a priori* judgement. He also argues that the omission of right acts is contrary to reason, i.e. that we have certain knowledge that right acts ought to be done; here is a second *a priori* judgement. Hume's consideration and rejection of these two views is complicated and even tortuous. He maintains that if Clarke is correct in asserting that moral conduct is based on *a priori* reasoning, then both arguments must be valid: we must know *a priori* both that certain acts are right and that right acts ought to be done. But Clarke, according to Hume, fails to show that we can make *a priori* judgements about either of these particulars.

Hencè Hume's argument falls into two parts.[1] He maintains first that to say of acts that they are right is not to say that they are fitting to a situation. Right is a term which Hume uses as synonymous with good, virtuous, and praiseworthy. Judgements about this characteristic are not, he thinks, about any relation in which acts stand to a situation, but are about the empirical fact that they are objects of valuation for an agent or a disinterested spectator. Hence judgements about rightness are not demonstrative. Secondly, Hume argues that even if

[1] See *Treatise*, ii, pp. 174, 175.

Clarke had succeeded in showing that rightness is a relation which can be the subject of *a priori* judgements, he would still not have been able to show that moral conduct rests on such judgements, for he did not and could not have succeeded in showing *a priori* that acts judged to be *right* are also *obligatory*. The latter of these two arguments is the more interesting and, from our point of view, the more important. But in Hume's criticism of Clarke they are so closely interwoven that we must offer some brief analysis of the first, in order that we may distinguish clearly between them.

Now, Hume begins his 'more particular argument' that 'the immutable fitnesses and unfitness of things cannot be defended by sound philosophy' in the following manner:

'There has been an opinion very industriously propagated by certain philosophers, that morality is susceptible of demonstration; and though no one has ever been able to advance a single step in those demonstrations, yet it is taken for granted that this science may be brought to an equal certainty with geometry or algebra. Upon this supposition, vice and virtue must consist in some relations; since it is allowed on all hands, that no matter of fact is capable of being demonstrated. Let us therefore begin by examining this hypothesis, and endeavour, if possible, to fix those moral qualities which have been so long the objects of our fruitless researches; point out distinctly the relations which constitute morality or obligation, that we may know wherein they consist, and after what manner we must judge them.'[1]

Now we might expect that Hume would follow up this passage with an analysis of Clarke's theory of moral relations. Clarke after all specified the relation between acts and situations which was, he thought, *par excellence* the moral relation as one of fittingness; and inadequate though this account of fittingness was, he did argue specifically that acts are right when they fit

[1] Ibid., p. 172. See also p. 166: 'Those who affirm that virtue is nothing but a conformity to reason; that there are eternal fitnesses and unfitnesses of things, which are the same to every rational being that considers them; that the immutable measure of right and wrong impose an obligation, not only on human creatures, but also on the Deity himself: all these systems concur in the opinion, that morality, like truth, is discerned merely by ideas, and by their juxtaposition and comparison.'

a situation in virtue of some agreement which they have with it. Fittingness is after all a common word, and it must have some connotation, though not perhaps one equal to Clarke's purpose.[1] Hence the least we are justified in expecting of Hume is a discussion of fittingness and agreement similar to that which we found in John Clarke and Hutcheson; but the *Treatise* contains no such discussion. In fact from this point on Hume writes as though Clarke had said no more than that rightness is some relational characteristic and had left the matter at that.

The reason for this is not far to seek. Hume clearly thought that Clarke's main object was to show that moral propositions are *a priori*, and that the theory of rightness as a relation of agreement holding between an act and a situation was introduced by him only because such a relation might be interpreted as a relation of agreement between ideas and hence that propositions about it might be *a priori*. For in Hume's view the only *a priori* propositions are those about relations between ideas. It seems it never occurred to Hume that Clarke might have been sincere in his attempt to analyse rightness in terms of fittingness and had only subsequently found that it followed from this analysis that moral propositions were *a priori*. Instead, Hume conceived of Clarke's whole relational theory simply as an edifice constructed to support the foregone conclusion that moral judgements are *a priori*. Clarke in fact, he thought, had an axe to grind, the axe that moral laws are demonstrable, and hence he treated Clarke's relational analysis of rightness in a very cursory manner. Whether Hume's attitude was justified or not is a difficult question. Certainly it was too radical in so far as Clarke does genuinely seem to have thought that rightness could be analysed in terms of fittingness, and this view seems to have been arrived at independently of any original belief that rightness is an *a priori* relation. On the other hand, it is true that even if this relational theory had been

---

[1] In fact Hume himself uses the word fitness and even refers to it as a relation. *Treatise*, ii, p. 206: 'It were better, no doubt, that every one were possessed of what is suitable to him, and proper for his use: But besides, that this relation of fitness . . .' and again, 'Justice, in her decisions, never regards the fitness or unfitness of objects to particular persons. . . .'

tenable, Clarke would still not have been justified in concluding that judgements about rightness are *a priori*, a conclusion
which he was all too anxious to draw. That Hume never took
this part of Clarke's theory seriously is evident from the footnote in which he writes:

'As a proof how confused our way of thinking on this subject commonly is, we may observe, that those who assert that morality is
demonstrable, do not say that morality lies in the relations, and that the
relations are distinguishable by reason. They only say that reason can
discover such an action, in such relations, to be virtuous, and such
another vicious. It seems they thought it sufficient if they could bring
the word Relation into the proposition, without troubling themselves
whether it was to the purpose or not. But here, I think, is plain argument. Demonstrative reason discovers only relations. But that reason,
according to this hypothesis, discovers also vice and virtue. These moral
qualities, therefore, must be relations. When we blame any action, in
any situation, the whole complicated object of action and situation must
form certain relations, wherein the essence of vice consists. This
hypothesis is not otherwise intelligible.'[1]

Thus it is that Hume neglects altogether Clarke's analysis of
moral rightness in terms of fittingness and proceeds as if Clarke
had said no more than that moral rightness is some unspecified
relation between an act and a situation. He contents himself
with pointing out that rightness or virtue is no *a priori* relation
known to him and with indicating certain conditions which
any relation which could be called moral would have to fulfil.

In writing as though Clarke had not specified the relation
of rightness Hume was not doing him justice, but Hume's main
argument is unaffected by this neglect, since his interest lay
not in showing merely that Clarke had failed to find an *a priori*
moral relation, but that the existence of such a relation was
unlikely if not impossible. Hume himself had certain precon-
ceptions about *a priori* relations. There were, he thought, only
four of these, 'resemblance, contrariety, degrees of quality, and
proportions of quantity and number',[2] and in criticizing Clarke
here he was not on firm ground, for his own theory of such
relations had very great weaknesses. In fact, according to his

[1] Ibid., p. 173.      [2] Ibid., i, p. 74.

general criterion, propositions about fittingness would have been *a priori*.[1] Yet he was right in arguing that Clarke himself had not produced a single argument to show that this was the case. In fact, as we have seen, on any intelligible view of *a priori* judgements, whether these propositions are demonstrable or not depends on the terms between which the relation of fittingness is supposed to hold.[2] Hume's argument here then is of a rather sweeping kind: 'If you assert that vice and virtue consist in relations susceptible of certainty and demonstration, you must confine yourself to those *four* relations which alone admit of that degree of evidence.'[3] But, he argues, it can be none of these, and

'Should it be asserted, that the sense of morality consists in the discovery of some relation distinct from these, . . . to this I know not what to reply, till someone be so good as to point out to me this new relation. It is impossible to refute a system which has never yet been explained. In such a manner of fighting in the dark, a man looses his blows in the air, and often places them where the enemy is not present.'[4]

Although Hume argues that he cannot refute the Clarkian view that moral relations are demonstrable until the relation which is supposed to be both moral and demonstrable has been specified, yet he does think that no one will ever be able to specify such relations. If there is a specifically moral relation, which is an independent characteristic of acts, it must as such be distinct from all similar non-moral ones. It would have to obtain in all cases where we speak of moral rightness and in none where we do not. Now, according to Clarke moral right-

---

[1] According to Hume a judgement about a relation is certain when the relation is such that our knowledge of it can be derived from the consideration of ideas alone. This view presents serious difficulties which cannot be discussed here. But we may note that according to Hume we can, for instance, know for certain that *x* is a darker blue than *y* because this relation follows from the natures of *x* and *y* when these ideas are given. On the other hand, we cannot know for certain that *x* is to the left of *y*, for there is nothing about the two ideas in themselves from which this relation could follow. But if we accept this view, then contrary to Hume's opinion we can know for certain that *x* fits *y* or does not fit *y*. For, just as it follows from my ideas of two blue objects that the one is darker than the other, so it follows from my idea of a kettle and of a kettle lid that if they were put together they would form a spatial whole.

[2] See above, p. 28.          [3] *Treatise*, ii, p. 172.          [4] Ibid., p. 173.

ness is a relation which obtains only between acts and situations, but it is, Hume thinks, unlikely that any relation can be so confined,

'. . . as moral good and evil belong only to the actions of the mind, and are derived from our situation with regard to external objects, the relations from which these moral distinctions arise must lie only betwixt internal actions and external objects, and must not be applicable either to internal actions, compared among themselves, or to external objects, when placed in opposition to other external objects.'[1]

It seems clear that Hume is not suggesting that a moral relation must possess the characteristic of obtaining only between these two things, but only that this is a condition demanded by Clarke's system, for Clarke thought that it was only to acts viewed in relation to the situation in which they occur that the term 'moral rightness' could be applied. If the relation of moral rightness were not of this exclusive kind, but could obtain also between acts of the mind when compared with one another, 'it would follow that we might be guilty of crimes within ourselves';[1] and, if the relation could obtain between external objects, it would follow that they also could be termed virtuous and vicious. These consequences would certainly be inconvenient for Clarke; but others, as indeed Hume himself, would find nothing curious in men being guilty of crimes within themselves, or in things other than acts being denominated virtuous and vicious. It seems that, so far from asserting that for anyone who wishes to show that moral rightness is a relation it is necessary to discover a relation which holds only between acts and situations, he is only pointing out that this is necessary for Clarke and at the same time obliquely exposing another of Clarke's absurdities, namely that according to him we cannot be guilty of crimes independently of our relation to external situations. Hume himself generally takes the view that rightness and virtuousness are attributable not so much to acts as to states of mind and character dispositions, and that they are attributable to them whatever external conditions prevail.[2]

[1] Ibid.
[2] According to Hume men are virtuous if they have a disposition to do virtuous actions even though circumstances prevent these dispositions from

For Clarke, however, it was necessary that the relation of moral rightness should obtain only between acts and situations, and Hume regarded this as an insuperable difficulty,

'. . . it seems difficult to imagine that any relation can be discovered betwixt our passions, volitions, and actions, compared to external objects, which relation might not belong either to these passions and volitions or to these external objects, compared among *themselves*.'[1]

Certainly the four *a priori* relations with which he was familiar were 'applicable not only to irrational but also to inanimate objects'.

Hume, however, was not content to leave his argument here. He goes on to consider examples of acts commonly called virtuous and shows that these acts have no *relational* characteristics different from those of morally indifferent events. He takes first the act of parricide and argues that the relations are the same when the human child kills his parent and when the sapling oak crowds out and kills the tree from whose seed it sprung. Next he considers incest and remarks that this is not considered vicious among animals, though here too the relations are the same as between rational beings. In the case of parricide

'It is', he argues, 'not sufficient to reply, that a choice or will is wanting. For in the case of parricide, a will does not give rise to any *different* relations, but is only the cause from which the action is derived; and consequently produces the *same* relations, that in the oak or elm arise from some other principles. It is a will or choice that determines a man to kill his parent: and they are the laws of matter and motion that determine a sapling to destroy the oak from which it sprung. Here then the same relations have different causes; but still the relations are the same: and as their discovery is not in both cases attended with the notion of immorality, it follows, that that notion does not arise from such a discovery.'[2]

Hume put forward this argument very forcefully, and evidently he was himself well pleased with it, for he concluded,

---

ever exerting themselves in action. See *Treatise*, ii, p. 280: 'Virtue in rags is still virtue; and the love which it procures attends a man into a dungeon or desert, where the virtue can no longer be exerted in action, and is lost to all the world.'

[1] Ibid., p. 174.        [2] Ibid., p. 175.

'This argument deserves to be weighed, as being, in my opinion, entirely decisive.'[1] But forceful though it is, it is not conclusive. It exposes the vagueness and inadequacy of Clarke's view, but it by no means shows that acts cannot have a special moral rightness which is a relational characteristic. Such moral rightness need not consist in a special relation; it might well be a wider relation obtaining between special things. More things are fitting than can be called morally right, and it seems difficult to imagine a special sort of fittingness—there cannot be different kinds of fittingness any more than there can be different kinds of causality or of identity[2]—but there is no reason why the fittingness between certain special things—such, for example, as that between human actions and the ends or expectations of sentient beings—might not be called moral rightness. This possibility Hume overlooked entirely, though he is to be excused for his negligence in that Clarke overlooked it also. If Hume failed to see how Clarke's view could be developed and made consistent, this was certainly in part Clarke's fault, for his view, as he stated it, was susceptible to all Hume's criticisms. Hence we can conclude that although Hume does not specifically prove that judgements about moral rightness cannot possibly be *a priori*, yet he is surely right in maintaining that the *onus probandi* rests with those who claim that they can, and that Clarke and his followers did not substantiate their claim. For they showed neither that the relation of moral rightness is *a priori*, nor even in what it consists.

It is important to separate this part of Hume's argument from the further observations with which he attempts to clinch his point. These observations are concerned with the meaning which Hume himself proposes to give to the term 'rightness' or 'virtuousness'. In his view this term does not signify any characteristic which actions possess in themselves. What it really signifies is a relation in which actions stand to an observer who contemplates them. To say that an act is right or

---

[1] Ibid., p. 176.
[2] It seems that different species of one and the same relation can only depend on differences between the things which are related and not to differences in the way in which they are related.

virtuous is to say that it is an object of approval; to say that it is wrong or vicious, that it is an object of disapproval.

'The vice entirely escapes you, as long as you consider the object. You never can find it, till you turn your reflection into your own breast, and find a sentiment of disapprobation, which arises in you, towards this action. . . . So that when you pronounce any action or character to be vicious, you mean nothing, but that from the constitution of your own nature you have a feeling or sentiment of blame from the contemplation of it.'[1]

He goes on to compare vice and virtue to the 'secondary qualities':

'Vice and virtue, therefore, may be compared to sounds, colours, heat, and cold, which, according to modern philosophy, are not qualities in objects, but perceptions in the mind: and this discovery in morals, like that other in physics, is to be regarded as a considerable advancement of the speculative sciences. . . .'[2]

Hume is here concerned to show that when we speak of acts as morally right or wrong, virtuous or vicious, we attribute to them a characteristic which they possess only in relation to the attitude or feelings of an observer; and from this he concludes once again that judgements about rightness or wrongness, virtue or vice, cannot be *a priori*.

Now, I think the acceptance of this view is not a necessary condition of the acceptance of Hume's earlier arguments against Clarke. The value of those arguments was, as we have seen, mainly negative; it consisted in Hume's insistence that judgements about rightness, if considered as judgements about an independent characteristic of actions, could not be assumed to be *a priori* without further proof; and this insistence remains of value even if we disagree with Hume's particular view that judgements about rightness cannot be *a priori* because they are about a relation between actions and the attitude or feelings of an observer. For it may well be that Hume was wrong in denying the existence of an independent rightness of actions, but right in denying that this relation can be the subject of *a priori* judgements.

[1] *Treatise*, ii, p. 177.                    [2] Ibid.

However, this is not the place to say more about this question. For we are here concerned with Hume's views on the demonstrability of *moral* judgements, and there is a narrower and more fundamental sense in which Hume uses the term 'moral', a sense in accordance with which judgements about rightness—either in Clarke's or in Hume's own use of this term—are not, properly speaking, *moral* judgements at all. There are passages where Hume insists that moral judgements—if indeed there are any—are about *obligations*, and in which he maintains that to assert of an agent that he has an obligation is essentially different from asserting of an action that it is right or virtuous. It is true Hume does not always consistently adhere to this usage, and there are many places, particularly in the later parts of the *Treatise*, where he identifies moral judgements with judgements of approval. But his narrower use of the term 'moral' is predominant in the later sections of Book II and the earlier sections of Book III, and it is on his acceptance of this usage of the term that his second major argument against the Clarkians rests.

We recalled at the beginning of this chapter that the Clarkian doctrine implied two contentions: the one that judgements about rightness or fittingness, the other that judgements about the obligation to do right or fitting acts, are *a priori*. Hume's second major argument against the *a priori* school is a criticism of this latter view. It is here that he maintains most firmly that assertions about the rightness or virtuousness of actions are distinct from assertions about obligations; and what he attempts to show is that, even if judgements about rightness were demonstrable, this would not entail that judgements about obligations must be demonstrable also; and furthermore, that it is in the nature of obligation that judgements about it could not possibly be *a priori*. This argument is advanced with great clarity in a passage which has attracted all too little attention, and which must be quoted at length:

'According to the principles of those who maintain an abstract rational difference betwixt moral good and evil, and a natural fitness and unfitness of things, it is not only supposed, that these relations, being eternal and immutable, are the same, when considered by every rational creature, but their *effects* are also supposed to be necessarily the same; and it is concluded they have no less, or rather a greater, influence in directing the will of the Deity, than in governing the rational and virtuous of our own species. These two particulars are evidently distinct. It is one thing to know virtue, and another to conform the will to it. In order, therefore, to prove that the measures of right and wrong are eternal laws, *obligatory* on every rational mind, it is not sufficient to show the relations upon which they are founded: we must also point out the connection betwixt the relation and the will; and must prove that this connection is so necessary, that in every well-disposed mind, it must take place and have its influence; though the difference betwixt these minds be in other respects immense and infinite. Now, besides what I have already proved, that even in human nature no relation can ever alone produce any action; besides this, I say, it has been shown, in treating of the understanding, that there is no connection of cause and effect, such as this is supposed to be, which is discoverable otherwise than by experience, and of which we can pretend to have any security by the simple consideration of the objects. All beings in the universe, considered in themselves, appear entirely loose and independent of each other. It is only by experience we learn their influence and connection; and this influence we ought never to extend beyond experience.

'Thus it will be impossible to fulfil the *first* condition required to the system of eternal rational measures of right and wrong; because it is impossible to show those relations, upon which such a distinction may be founded: and it is as impossible to fulfil the *second* condition; because we cannot prove *a priori*, that these relations, if they really existed and were perceived, would be universally forcible and obligatory.'[1]

Hume's first point in this passage is that to show that acts are right is not *ipso facto* to show that they are obligatory. To say that an act is right is, according to Clarke, to say that it will, when it occurs, stand in a certain relation to the situation in which it occurs, and, according to Hume, to say that it will evoke certain feelings of approval in the agent or spectator. But to say that it is obligatory is quite another thing. It is not to say that an act will have certain characteristics when it is done; or even that it would have these characteristics if it were

---

[1] *Treatise*, ii, p. 174.

done. It is to say that somebody ought to do it. This is a statement about the doing of the act and cannot, according to Hume, be deduced from anything about its nature. 'In order . . . to prove that the measures of right and wrong are eternal laws, "obligatory" on every rational mind, it is not sufficient to show the relations upon which they are founded. . . .' Hume prints obligatory in italics, though he uses italics far more sparingly than the majority of eighteenth-century philosophers. To this passage he adds, at the end of the section, a further remark which clinches his argument:

'In every system of morality which I have hitherto met with, I have always remarked, that the author proceeds for some time in the ordinary way of reasoning, and establishes the being of God, or makes observations concerning human affairs; when of a sudden I am surprised to find, that instead of the usual copulations of propositions, *is*, and *is not*, I meet with no proposition that is not connected with an *ought*, or an *ought not*. This change is imperceptible; but is, however, of the last consequence. For as this *ought*, or *ought not*, expresses some new relation or affirmation, it is necessary that it should be observed and explained; and at the same time, that a reason should be given, for what seems altogether inconceivable, how this new relation can be a deduction from others, which are entirely different from it.'[1]

This argument is of great merit. Evidently to say that an act is obligatory is to make some statement about a relation between an agent and the doing of the action, and is therefore quite distinct from saying that the act itself when it occurs will be of a certain kind or will stand in a certain relation to a situation. Hence propositions about obligation cannot be reduced to propositions about the rightness or virtuousness of actions. The statement that an agent is obliged to do an act can never be transcribed into one which omits all reference to the agent. Nor does it seem possible to say that a proposition about an agent being obliged can ever be entailed by one about an act's being right.[2] We cannot conclude from our knowledge that an act is of a certain kind anything about an agent's relation

[1] Ibid. p. 177.
[2] Unless of course by a 'morally right act' is meant no more than an act which is conformable to what we ought to do.

to the doing of it. To say that an act is obligatory is not to say that it is right or good or virtuous, but that someone is obliged to do it, and there is no verb 'righted' or 'gooded' which can be used to replace 'obliged'. With this part of Hume's argument it seems we must agree; even Clarke, as we have seen, did not always maintain that for an act to be right or fitting is the same as for an agent to be obliged to do it. Sometimes, at any rate, he seems to have regarded rightness or fittingness as the sole ground rather than as the essence of obligation. But which ever of these two views he took, Hume's criticism is fully justified. For whether Clarke overlooked the difference between rightness and obligation or not, Hume is right in saying that even if he had shown that propositions about *rightness* were demonstrable, this argument in itself would have shown nothing about the demonstrability of propositions about *obligation*.

But Hume's argument does not leave the matter here. He maintains not merely that obligation is a relation between an agent and the doing of an action, he also points out what kind of relation this is, in order to show that propositions about it are in principle incapable of demonstration. According to Hume, to say that an act is obligatory is to say something about a relation between the thought of it and an agent's *will*: it is to say that, in some manner, an agent is prompted to do an action by the thought of it. Hence, if reason is to show that certain acts are obligatory, it must provide the agent with motives for doing them. Moral judgements must in fact be such as to influence action; they must be *practical*.

The argument recurs many times in this part of the *Treatise* and is central to the whole of Hume's theory of obligation. Indeed in the second book, where Hume discusses the 'influencing motives of the will', he simply assumes that whatever makes us conscious of our obligations, whether reasoning or feeling, must affect what we do. After stating that in the common view this is the work of reason he goes on to argue that in order to show up the 'fallacy of all this philosophy' it is only necessary to show that 'reason alone can never be the motive to any action of the will'. Here he dispenses altogether with that step in the argument where it is asserted that whatever is the basis of morality must provide the agent with a motive. This argument, however, occurs in detail in Book III, where Hume writes that 'Philosophy is commonly divided into *speculative* and *practical*; and as morality is always comprehended under the latter division, it is supposed to influence our passions and actions, and to go beyond the calm and indolent judgements of the understanding';[1] and again, 'Morals excite passions, and produce or prevent actions'.[2] It is, he argues, commonly thought that an agent's opinion or belief that a certain act is his duty provides him with a *cause* for doing the act. To alter an agent's opinion about what it is that he ought to do is at the same time to provide him with impelling reasons for doing it, with reasons which can have a causal influence upon his subsequent behaviour. If moral arguments were not essentially of this kind they would be fruitless. As Hume puts it, 'If morality had naturally no influence on human passions and actions, it were in vain to take such pains to inculcate it; and nothing would be more fruitless than that multitude of rules and precepts with which moralists abound.'[3] He goes on to argue that we are in fact justified in this expectation; common experience '. . . informs us that men are often governed by their duties, and are deterred from some actions by the opinion of injustice, and impelled to others by that of obligation'.[4]

This argument is of fundamental importance. It is certainly true that we do regard our notions of morality as possessed of practical force, and that judgements about obligations, if indeed such judgements can ever be made, cannot leave us indifferent like the 'calm and indolent judgements of the understanding'; they must, like Hutcheson's 'exciting reasons', be capable of having practical effect. Clarke, as we have seen, was not wholly oblivious to this fact. Indeed he regarded morality as having great influence though he did not grasp the implications of this view, i.e. that moral judgements must be practical.

---

[1] *Treatise*, ii, p. 166.  [2] Ibid., p. 167.
[3] Ibid., p. 166.  [4] Ibid., p. 167.

Hume himself regards Clarke as aware of the practical nature of morality, though quite unaware of the difficulties involved in maintaining this view side by side with the theory that moral conduct is based on *a priori* judgements. As we saw in the passage quoted above, he argues that, 'According to those who maintain an abstract rational difference betwixt moral good and evil', it is not only argued that these relations are the same for all rational creatures, 'but their *effects* are also supposed to be necessarily the same; and it is concluded they have no less, or rather a greater, influence in directing the will of the Deity, than in governing the rational and virtuous of our own species'. But, Hume maintains, relational propositions about rightness, even if there were propositions of this kind, would not be practical. A judgement about obligation must in some degree affect our being moved to act, while judgements about rightness or virtue need not: 'it is one thing to know virtue and another to conform the will to it'. Hence, even if it were the case that we are always obliged to do right acts and right acts only, a judgement about obligation would still only be that which asserted a connexion between this 'relation and the will' —but, Hume concludes, such a judgement cannot be universal and necessary. For a judgement about the connexion which links the thought of an action which has a certain relational property to an agent's will is a causal judgement; and, in accordance with Hume's general principles, no causal judgement can be universal and necessary. With this argument we shall be concerned in detail in the next chapter; it is only mentioned here because it occurs in the passage where he argues that judgements about obligations must be practical, a passage which would be incomplete without this conclusion.[1]

[1] It is interesting to notice that Hume advances a similar argument against Wollaston. To show that acts give rise to false conclusions in others cannot be to show that they are immoral. For, he says, unless we thought such acts immoral on other grounds we should never be led to avoid them: '. . . if there be not an evident merit or turpitude annexed to this species of truth or falsehood, it can never have any influence upon our actions. For whoever thought of forbearing any action, because others might possibly draw false conclusions from it? Or whoever performed any, that he might give rise to true conclusions?' *Treatise*, ii, p. 171.

Hume, then, has two arguments about the nature of moral judgements in the more narrow sense. First, they are judgements about an agent's obligation to action, and, as such, they differ from all judgements about the nature of actions, about their rightness, goodness, or virtuousness.[1] Secondly, as judgements about obligations, they are practical judgements, that is, judgements which essentially have some effect on the agent's will. Of course, Hume does not argue that we are obliged whenever we are moved, or that all practical judgements are moral ones; but he does maintain that to be obliged is to be moved, and that if there are moral judgements they must be practical.

The first part of this argument, as we have said, seems inescapable, but there are many who would disagree with the second. Such an argument would be opposed by all those who maintain with Clarke that what we are obliged to do are acts simply because they have certain characteristics independently of the impelling force of the thought of them, e.g. independent of our attitude towards being right, or conducive to good or to happiness. Yet Hume makes his point so forcefully that it is hard to see how his conclusions can be avoided. Anybody who argues against him that to be obliged is not in some special manner to be moved, and that reason in showing that men are obliged does not show in what direction they would have to be moved, but something else, is faced with two difficulties which appear to be insurmountable. He has to assume both that when we argue with men that it is their duty to do certain acts, we do not do so with a view to influencing their conduct, and that men can have obligations which it is out of their power to fulfil. Neither of these assumptions appears justified. It is a fact that when we argue with $x$ that he is obliged to do $y$, we do think that, if we succeed in making him agree with us that $y$ is his duty, we shall have provided him with a motive for doing $y$. Hume is right: if this were not the case there would be no point in arguing about obligations. Furthermore, it would be very odd to say that men are under obligations to do acts which they

[1] See W. D. Falk, 'Obligation and Rightness', *Philosophy*, July 1945.

cannot possibly do, yet they cannot do acts which they are not moved to do, for an action without a motive impelling to do it is inconceivable. It is difficult to see what can be meant by being obliged, if it is denied that it is *ipso facto* being under the influence of a motive which both prompts and enables us to do what we are obliged to do. What the state of being obliged would then be is quite unimaginable, and it would certainly be very far removed from anything which this phrase means in common speech. In Hume's words, 'No action can be required of us as our duty, unless there be implanted in human nature some actuating passion or motive capable of producing the action.'[1]

From all this it follows that if reason or judgement is to be an essential prerequisite of moral conduct it must be shown that reason or judgement, either empirical or *a priori*, can influence conduct. Hence the question of whether practical judgements are possible, and if so whether that particular kind of practical judgement which can be called moral is possible, becomes for Hume the touchstone of the problem of rationalism in ethics. To show that such judgements are possible is essential for anybody who wishes to maintain that reason is the foundation of moral conduct. It was the great merit of Hume as a moral philosopher that he distilled this from the seventeenth- and early eighteenth-century controversies as the crucial problem. It is true that later in the *Treatise* and in the *Inquiry* he in some degree loses sight of the problem of obligation and becomes absorbed in the problems of virtue and valuation, but before this point is reached he has a great deal to say about obligation and practical judgements, that is, the problem whether reason can influence conduct.

Whether or not Hume thought that there was a special class of practical judgements which could be called moral is not for us to consider now. This question must be left open until we have discussed all that he has to say about practical judgements in general. We have therefore to consider in detail in the

---

[1] See *Treatise*, ii, p. 221.

subsequent chapters Hume's answers to the three all-important questions in the following order: (i) Can demonstrative reasoning influence conduct; are there any *a priori* practical judgements? (ii) Can empirical reasoning influence conduct; can it make practical judgements? (iii) Can reasoning influence moral conduct; are there any specially moral practical judgements? The answers to these three questions are of central importance for moral philosophy, and Hume's attempts to answer them, though not altogether satisfactory, throw a great deal of light on the nature of moral obligation.

# CHAPTER III

# DEMONSTRATIVE REASON AND CONDUCT

WE come now to consider Hume's views on the limits within which demonstrative reasoning can influence conduct. The view, not merely that demonstrative reasoning has such an influence, but that this influence is a very considerable one was, as we have seen, widely held during the seventeenth and eighteenth centuries. Thus Hobbes had said that 'injustice' was 'absurdity in conversation', and Clarke that 'iniquity' was 'the very same in action as falsity and contradiction in theory'. Clarke thought that it was self-contradictory knowingly to will unfitting acts, and Wollaston that it was self-contradictory to will acts which 'assert' falsehoods. They all agreed in thinking that some acts were self-contradictory and others logically necessary, and that the discovery of certain relations of implication was in itself sufficient to alter the course of human action. They thought that, as the result of making *a priori* judgements, men would be moved to do some acts to which they would otherwise have been indifferent, and to refrain from others which previously they had been ready to perform. It is with the examination and refutation of this view that Hume is largely concerned, both in the book *Of the Passions*, in the section entitled 'Of the Influencing Motives of the Will', and in the book *Of Morals*, in the section, 'Moral Distinctions not Derived from Reason'.

From a superficial reading of these sections we might conclude that Hume's answer to the question: Can *a priori* reasoning influence action, was wholly negative. Yet this is not the case. In fact he has two arguments. On the one hand, he admits that there is a way in which demonstrative reasoning can influence conduct, but that there its influence is only *indirect* and *oblique*; and, on the other, he argues that this is the *only* influence which such reasoning can have. The *direct* and *immediate* influence which the Clarkians ascribed to reasoning, and on which the validity of their moral theory depends, is according to Hume altogether impossible. We must consider these two arguments separately. Let us take first the view that *a priori* judgements *can* have an indirect influence.

Hume begins his argument in the section 'Of the Influencing Motives of the Will' with the remark that, in order to show up the fallacy of supposing that there is a combat between reason and passion and that reason has pre-eminence over passion, he will 'endeavour to prove *first*, that reason alone can never be a motive to any action of the will; and *secondly*, that it can never oppose passion in the direction of the will'.[1] He then proceeds to consider the possible influence of judgements about the 'abstract relations of our ideas'. His argument here is that 'abstract and demonstrative reasoning' influences action only by 'directing our judgements concerning causes and effects'. He gives as an example of such reasoning the making of mathematical judgements.

'Mathematics, indeed, are useful in all mechanical operations, and arithmetic in almost every art and profession: but it is not of themselves they have any influence. Mechanics are the art of regulating the motions of bodies *to some designed end or purpose*; and the reason why we employ arithmetic in fixing the proportions of numbers, is only that we may discover the proportions of their influence and operation.'

Of this influence he gives a more precise example:

'A merchant is desirous of knowing the sum total of his accounts with any person: why? but that he may learn what sum will have the same *effects* in paying his debt, and going to market, as all the particular articles taken together.'[2]

Here, unfortunately, Hume's exposition of the way in which demonstrative judgements can affect action comes to an end. He goes on to argue that demonstrative reasoning cannot affect action in any other way, and to consider the effects of empirical reasoning, both of which arguments we will consider later. It seems that he introduces the above argument about the indirect effect of demonstrative judgements not because he is particularly interested in the fact that such judgements do influence our actions in this way, but rather in order to make it plain

[1] *Treatise*, ii, p. 126.          [2] Ibid.

that in denying that they have any influence of a more direct kind he is not also denying the influence which he here ascribes to them; and further, in order to make it plain that this influence is only oblique and indirect, that 'it is not of themselves that they [judgements] have influence'. His argument, however, is of considerable consequence. It is important both in relation to his refutation of the doctrines of the *a priori* school, and in relation to his own positive theory. We have, therefore, to fill in for ourselves the detail which is implied by Hume's argument, but which he himself omitted. Precisely what sort of judgements had he in mind, and what exactly did he mean by saying that 'it is not in themselves that they have influence'?

It is evident from the context that Hume is here referring to all ordinary *a priori* judgements. His specific reference is to mathematical judgements, but we can assume that he had also other such judgements in mind. His argument then is that the making of judgements like 'two plus two is equal to four', 'deaf men cannot overhear what is said', and 'fierce dogs are apt to bite' may at times cause us to be affected by the thought of actions which would otherwise have left us indifferent. But he argues, the effects of such judgements depend on certain empirical conditions being given. They have influence only in so far as they show that $x$ has by implication a property $y$ which is already desired. Thus Hume's merchant is already desirous of paying his debts; that is to say, he is moved by the thought of paying a certain sum of money which is equal to the sum total of his debts. He then makes certain mathematical judgements with a view to discovering what this sum is expressed in terms of pounds, shillings, and pence; by adding various quantities together he discovers that the sum he owes is, say, £150. This judgement arouses in him the desire to pay £150; a desire which he did not feel before he had made the calculation, since the exact quantity of his debts was then unknown to him. Similarly, a man who does not like being overheard, but wants to employ a servant, and consequently wants to employ a man who will not overhear anything, can be influenced by the judgement that 'deaf men cannot eavesdrop';

as the result of this judgement he may come into the state of being moved by the thought of employing a deaf man. Again, a man who wants to buy a dog, but does not like being bitten, and who is offered a dog with a reputation for fierceness, will be influenced by the judgement 'fierce dogs are apt to bite'. In all these cases a certain desire is presupposed, a desire to pay that sum of money which is equal to the total of a debt, to employ that man who will not eavesdrop, to buy that dog which will not bite. The *a priori* judgements which are effective in these conditions are those by which certain objects are identified as objects of these descriptions. They are the judgements which show *what* sum of money is equivalent to the sum total of a debt, *what* man will not eavesdrop, *what* dog will not bite.

To this it may be objected that many *a priori* judgements are trifling and do not have any effect. This, of course, is true. If I want a black cat, I shall not be affected in my choice of cats by the judgement that 'black cats are cats which are black', for black cats and cats which are black are already identified in my mind. The same may be true in the last of the cases mentioned above; fierce dogs may be identified with dogs that are apt to bite, without any special judgement of identification. On the other hand, there are many cases where identification does not take place without judgement. I do not immediately think of a deaf man as a man who will not eavesdrop. But there is no doubt much significance in Hume's choice of a mathematical example; the great majority of *a priori* judgements which indirectly affect our actions are clearly of this kind. The merchant could never identify the sum total of his debts with £150 without making a specific judgement, because without such a judgement it is, for instance, impossible to see that £19 plus £49 plus £36 plus £46 is identical with £150. In order to recognize the extent of the influence of mathematical judgements it is necessary only to consider the construction of any elaborate piece of machinery. Not only very many physical parts but also very many mathematical judgements go into the construction of a modern aeroplane. Without such judgements our actions in making the aeroplane would have been very different from what they in fact are.

Yet despite the obvious effect of such judgements, Hume is right in arguing that 'it is not of themselves that they have influence'. In all these cases the action is directly caused not by the judgement which discovers the act to possess some characteristic which is already desired, but by the fact that an object with these characteristics was already an object of desire. The actions which we do as the result of such demonstrative reasoning, no less than those which we do independently of judgement, are *immediately* caused by desire—or rather they are caused by the thought of objects which arouse desire, either because they are attended by feelings of pleasure, or because they appeal to some instinctive disposition which cannot be further explained.[1] In so far as we can say that these actions are caused by judgement we mean only that they are 'mediately' or 'obliquely' so caused.

From the argument that demonstrative reasoning alone cannot cause action Hume concludes that this reasoning alone also cannot prevent action. If I desire to pay my creditor £170 when my debts to him are in fact only £150, my judgement that they are only £150 may indeed prevent me from paying the larger amount, but it will only do so because my first desire is to pay him the sum total of my debts. The desire to pay £170 was not an original desire, it arose only as the result of a false judgement. The new judgement that my debts amount not to £170 but to £150 will affect my action, but only because in making it I recognize that the amount which I desire to pay is other than what I had previously taken it to be.

Hume's argument then is that demonstrative reasoning has some effect in causing and preventing action; but he thinks that, since this effect is only a mediate one, we are not on this account entitled to speak of acts as *a priori* reasonable and un-

[1] See *Treatise*, ii, p. 148: '*Desire* arises from good considered simply. . . . Besides good and evil, or, in other words, pain and pleasure, the direct passions frequently arise from a natural impulse or instinct, which is perfectly unaccountable. Of this kind is the desire of punishment to our enemies, and of happiness to our friends; hunger, lust, and a few other bodily appetites.'

reasonable. It would be unreasonable to judge that 'employing deaf men is employing men who are able to overhear what is said', but it would be only in an 'oblique' and 'unphilosophical' sense that, by transferring the epithet unreasonable from the false judgement to the action resulting from it, we could say 'it is unreasonable not to employ, or not to want to employ, a deaf man.' '. . . a passion', Hume writes, 'must be accompanied with some false judgement, in order to its being unreasonable; and even then it is not the passion, properly speaking, which is unreasonable, but the judgement.'[1]

With this verdict we must agree. It is true that our passions are sometimes influenced by demonstrative judgements, and that we try to affect others by *a priori* arguments. But our judgements and arguments in these cases are not about the falseness of some proposed course of action, or the unreasonableness of some desire, but about the falseness or inadequacy of the judgements by which these desires are directed. To the merchant who is about to hand over £170, when his debts amount only to £150, we point out that his calculations are mistaken. To the man who is about to employ a deaf servant we say: 'True, a deaf servant will not overhear what you say, but on the other hand, he will also be incapable of answering the telephone.' And with the man who has decided not to buy a fierce dog we argue: 'Fierce dogs are as apt to bite burglars as their owners.' We think that by pointing out these relations and changing or supplementing the judgements of the agent we shall also succeed in changing his desires and hence in affecting his actions. But our arguments here are all about the validity or adequacy of his previous judgements and not about the desires and actions which we expect to follow from them. The demonstrative reasoning which we have been considering does no more than establish relations between ideas; it does not establish any relations between these ideas and the agent's passions, volitions, and actions; and this is after all what is to be expected, for, as Hume points out, the 'proper province' of such reasoning 'is the world of ideas, and as the will always

[1] Ibid., p. 128.

places us in that of realities, demonstration and volition seem upon that account to be totally removed from each other'.[1] We have therefore to agree with Hume's conclusion that demonstrative reasoning alone is 'perfectly inert'. It is possible to make any of the judgements which we have been considering without being affected by them, for they cannot affect us unless our desires are already concerned with the objects which they are about.[2]

Such is the first of Hume's arguments about the relation between demonstrative reasoning and conduct, but, as we have already indicated, it is not his only argument. The 'opinion' that demonstrative reasoning has only an indirect effect 'may', he says, 'appear somewhat extraordinary, and it may not be improper to confirm it by some other considerations'.[3] These 'other considerations' appear both in the section 'Of the Influencing Motives of the Will' and in the section 'Moral Distinctions not Derived from Reason', and in the latter they are accompanied by yet another argument.

Now the 'other considerations' together with the further argument are really about a problem different from that with which Hume has so far been concerned. For previously his problem was that of the influence of ordinary demonstrative judgements, judgements identifying objects already desired as being objects of a certain kind. But in these 'other considerations' he is concerned with judgements of a peculiar kind, those which are themselves *about* the 'passions, volitions, and actions' that they are supposed to influence. In the previous argument Hume was concerned to show that demonstrative judgements about objects can only influence actions indirectly, but here he sets out to prove that judgements about 'passions, volitions, and actions', which might in some sense influence conduct *directly*, cannot be demonstrative. Desiring, willing, and acting, he

---

[1] *Treatise*, ii, p. 126.

[2] There is, as we shall see later, a further reason why such judgements need not necessarily influence action. That is that, even though we may desire an act which these judgements identify as being of a certain kind, it does not follow that we shall desire this act, for our desires may remain dissociated from this judgement.          [3] Ibid., p. 127.

argues, can never be self-contradictory or logically necessary, and hence no judgements about this contradiction or necessity can affect our conduct.

Hume himself does not explain his reasons for introducing this new problem. Yet his arguments here are of the greatest importance. For clearly no analysis of the practical influence of *a priori* reason would be complete if it did not take account of the question, Are demonstrative judgements about the necessity of desiring or willing certain actions possible? Moreover, without a consideration of this problem his refutation of the *a priori* school would have been inadequate, for he would then have ignored one of their most important arguments. In order, therefore, to understand the full significance of Hume's 'other considerations' it is necessary to consider the reasons for introducing them a little further.

If we recall for a moment the doctrine of the *a priori* moralists, we shall see that Hume's previous argument has disposed of only part of it. It is true that Clarke, and all the other members of this school who identified moral with fitting actions, sometimes contended that judgements about the fittingness of acts (which, as we have seen, they thought to be *a priori*) were in themselves sufficient to prompt agents to do those acts which they showed to be fitting.[1] Hume's first argument was sufficient to answer this view, and it is true, indeed, that he met it also on other grounds; for he contended, as we have seen, that judgements about fittingness are not in any case *a priori*, but his argument that the effect of *a priori* judgements is always indirect and oblique added weight to this by showing that judgements about fittingness, whether *a priori* or empirical, could not have that practical influence which the Clarkians allotted to them. The judgement that 'charitableness is fitting' has just as much and just as little effect, as the judgement that 'deaf men cannot answer the telephone'. Granted a desire to employ a man who can answer the telephone, in the one case, and a desire to do fitting acts in the other, these judgements can direct our desires towards the specific acts of employing

[1] See above, pp. 28 ff.

men who are not deaf, and doing what is charitable. But if these desires are not presupposed these judgements are quite powerless.

But the contention that judgements about fittingness alone are capable of causing actions was not the only argument with which the *a priori* school supported their view that demonstrative reasoning can control action. It is notable that this argument was in any case strictly Clarkian and was not used by Wollaston or by Hobbes. The main argument which all these philosophers relied on was not that *a priori* judgements about fittingness must themselves cause action, but that it is possible to make *a priori* judgements about the necessity of *willing* and of *doing* fitting acts. Granted that we already know a certain act to be fitting, it is, they argued, evident *a priori* that it is unreasonable not to do this act, for the judgement that it is reasonable to omit it, or, as they sometimes said, the omitting itself, is self-contradictory; 'Tis as absurd wilfully to act contrary to known justice and equity . . . that is to will things to be what they are not and cannot be, as it would be for a man in arithmetical matters ignorantly to believe twice two not equal to four.' Hume had therefore to show that Clarke and Wollaston were wrong in supposing that there can be *a priori* judgements of this kind.

But even if Hume had not been confronted with the Clarkian theory, the question of the demonstrability of judgements about 'passions, volitions, and actions' would still have been of paramount importance for his argument. Had he not considered this problem, his whole treatment of the practical influence of demonstrative reasoning would have been incomplete. For though it must be granted that when we speak of such influence we do often refer to that of the judgements which Hume began by considering, yet it is evident that these are not the only sort of judgements which we normally consider to have practical influence. It is true that in trying to affect the actions of others we do employ arguments such as 'deaf men cannot answer the telephone' and 'fierce dogs are apt to bite burglars', but if these remarks have no effect we do not always leave the matter here.

To the man who is on the point of employing a deaf servant I may begin by pointing out the implications of his action, but if he remains unaffected by the statement of these implications I shall not be at a loss to find further ways of dissuading him from so foolish a course of action. On the contrary I shall continue my argument by saying, 'But surely, *since* deaf men cannot answer the telephone, you *cannot really want to employ a deaf man*'. We argue in this way with others. We do not merely make statements about the implications of proposed courses of action and leave the agent to draw his own conclusions. By stating that, on account of the agent's desires and the nature of the act, he *must* or *cannot really want* to do it, we point out the conclusion to him. In the same way, when we ourselves contemplate our future actions, we do not merely consider what these actions would be like if we did them, but also whether we really want to do them; we judge not merely that 'fierce dogs bite burglars', but that '*since* fierce dogs bite burglars, we *cannot but want* to keep a fierce dog'.

We shall have a great deal to say about such judgements in the next chapter, for there we will be concerned with Hume's analysis of the influence of *empirical* judgements on action, and when he comes to consider this influence he again takes account of the effects of the two different kinds of judgements. There he begins by considering the indirect influence of judgements like 'this fruit is ripe' and 'the only way to reach it is to climb a ladder', judgements in the empirical field whose influence offers a precise parallel to *a priori* judgements such as 'fierce dogs are apt to bite' and 'deaf men cannot answer the telephone'. But there also he is not merely concerned with judgements of this kind, but also with judgements which are themselves about the desiring, willing, and acting which they influence. It is not possible to consider the implications of the difference between these two kinds of judgements in detail until we have reviewed Hume's argument about the effects of empirical judgements; here it is sufficient to mention that they differ in two all-important respects, respects to which Hume never explicitly draws attention, but which are of paramount importance for his whole analysis of practical reason, and which must be borne in mind throughout the whole of the subsequent discussion. Judgements like 'You cannot *really* want to employ deaf men' differ from judgements like 'Deaf men cannot answer the telephone', first, in that they are about a *relation between an agent and the thought of an action*. In making such judgements we are not assenting to a proposition which states that an act *y* is of the kind *z*, but to one which states that on reflection an agent *must* or *must not* be moved by the thought of *y*. In this respect they are essentially different from all judgements which do not state anything about an agent's relation to an action, and we should expect this to have implications for the manner in which they influence action. This is in fact the case, for the second respect in which these judgements differ is that, while the effect of judgements about the nature of objects is merely *incidental* to the judgements themselves, the effect of judgements about what an agent must or must not do is *essential* to them. The judgement that 'fierce dogs are apt to bite burglars' may or may not influence action. Whether it does so or not depends partly on whether the agent is interested in burglars being bitten, and partly on whether he draws from this any conclusions about his own actions. That is to say, it is always possible to make this judgement and remain quite unaffected by it. Such judgements are, in Hume's words, 'calm and indolent judgements of the understanding'. But the judgement, 'I must on reflection want to buy a fierce dog', cannot leave me indifferent. I may of course entertain this proposition without assenting to it, or I may hear somebody else say that I must want to buy a fierce dog, but I cannot myself assent to this proposition as true, and at the same time not be moved by the thought of buying the dog. For, in verifying the proposition I cause myself to come into the very state of desiring that which the proposition asserts I should desire on reflection; if I did not I could not assent to the proposition as true. The making of judgements about what I really desire, or what I must desire on reflection, must by its very nature affect me whose desires it is about. The practical effect of such judgements is then essential and not merely incidental to them. We cannot make them and remain unmoved.

Throughout the rest of this book I shall refer to judgements whose practical effect is essential—a necessary consequence of their form—as *practical judgements*, and to those whose effect is not a necessary consequence of their form as *theoretical*. Hume does not himself use these terms. He refers to the latter as the 'calm and indolent judgements of the understanding', and to the former, in so far as he refers to them specifically at all, as judgements about the relation between an action and an agent's will. But the distinction between the two is so fundamental for the whole problem of the influence of reason on conduct that we must use separate words to denote judgements of the one and of the other kind.

In denying that judgements like 'Deaf men cannot answer the telephone' are practical judgements we are not denying that they can have practical influence. That they can have some practical influence is evident, and it is with Hume's consideration of this fact that we have so far been concerned. If we were to express Hume's argument in terms of practical and theoretical judgements we should say that there are *a priori* theoretical judgements which have practical influence, but that this does not imply that there are *a priori* practical judgements. The second part of Hume's argument, the 'other considerations', is concerned with the problem of whether practical judgements proper can be *a priori*. For this was the position that the Clarkians together with the other *a priori* moralists maintained.

It would, however, be misleading to suppose that either Clarke or Hume explicitly recognized the difference between theoretical and practical judgements. Clarke could not himself have attributed any very great significance to this distinction, for he mistakenly supposed that the practical effect of judgements about objects, equally with that of those about passions, volitions, and actions, was essential to them; it is in fact difficult to see precisely how he could have drawn this distinction. And Hume, although he answers Clarke's two arguments separately, writes as though he thought his answer to the second were no more than a further argument in support of his answer to the first. Moreover, Hume like Clarke, at any rate when considering *a priori* judgements. gives no precise description of what this second influence is. Clarke refers to the necessity of willing certain actions as a logical necessity. And Hume in countering this view contends that logical necessity does not pertain to 'passions, volitions, and actions'. Both arguments are in some respects vague; they are not explicitly about the question of whether propositions asserting that the thought of certain acts must move an agent are demonstrable. The class of judgements with which they are concerned is a wider class than that which comprises only practical judgements proper, for it is evident that many judgements about passions, volitions, and actions are not practical at all. If any action, passion, or volition is unconditionally impossible, then no judgement about this impossibility can influence such an action, passion, or volition. If it is impossible to do, will, or desire any act, then it is impossible to do, will or desire it, and judging that this is the case cannot bring me into a new state of doing, willing, or desiring, or of not doing, willing, or desiring it, for it follows that I never did do, will, or desire it, nor ever could. Moreover, granted that I am already moved by the thought of an act, the judgement that I am so moved will not affect me, for this judgement will only be true so long as I continue to be in the same state of being moved that I was in before I made the judgement. The only judgements which can properly be said to have a direct and essential effect on action are judgements about what *I should feel moved to do if I reflected.* For these do not assert that $x$ must unconditionally be the case; but that it would be the case if some further condition were fulfilled, and it is only when I set about verifying these judgements as being true of myself that this condition is fulfilled, and that the state of affairs which is asserted by the judgement in hypothetical form becomes actual.

Thus, we can see that both Clarke and Hume were concerned

with a wider field of judgements than those which can strictly be called practical. Nevertheless, there can be no doubt that, though their discussion was not limited to these judgements, it was these that they had in mind. Although Clarke thought that judgements about fittingness were also practical, he none the less distinguished between them and judgements about the necessity of acting. Further, his argument about the latter is not always that we cannot, or must, will or do certain acts, but sometimes that we cannot, or must, *knowingly* will or do them. He does not always speak of doing and willing as impossible in themselves, but he refers to them also as *morally* impossible, by which he evidently means that they are impossible for a rational agent who has in some way or other considered them. Moreover, it is clear that Hume when he argues that moral judgements, if there are any, must influence action is referring to the supposed influence of practical and not of theoretical judgements. For he allows, as we have seen, that even demonstrative reasoning can have an indirect effect on action, but he does not regard this effect as comparable to that which we would need to attribute to moral judgements. The practical influence of moral judgements would, he thinks, have to be essential and direct. From his denial that *a priori* judgements have a direct influence on action he concludes that 'as reason can never *immediately* prevent or produce any action by contradicting or approving of it, it cannot be the source of moral good and evil, which are found to have that influence'.[1] Clearly Hume is here referring to the essential influence which pertains to practical judgements; no other influence would fulfil his requirements.

With these preliminary remarks in mind we must now turn to Hume's 'other considerations'. His arguments here are trenchant, but they are very brief, and as they stand they are incomplete. The first argument is that 'passions, volitions, and actions' are real entities or, as Hume calls them, 'original facts and realities', and as such they are incapable of being called either reasonable or unreasonable. This argument is stated in

---

[1] *Treatise*, ii, p. 168 (my italics).

the following passage which occurs in the section 'Moral Distinctions not Derived from Reason':

'Reason is the discovery of truth or falsehood. Truth or falsehood consists in an agreement or disagreement either to the *real* relations of ideas, or to *real* existence and matter of fact. Whatever therefore is not susceptible of this agreement or disagreement, is incapable of being true or false, and can never be an object of our reason. Now, it is evident our passions, volitions, and actions, are not susceptible of any such agreement or disagreement; being original facts and realities, complete in themselves, and implying no reference to other passions, volitions, and actions. It is impossible, therefore, they can be pronounced either true or false, and be either contrary or conformable to reason.'[1]

Hume's second argument is that propositions about the motives which give rise to actions are *causal* propositions, and therefore cannot be *a priori*. This argument occurs in connexion with his contention that to be obliged is to be moved. It is expressed in a passage which we have already considered in the last chapter. It is, according to Hume, in principle impossible to say that the thought of any act is such that it must move the agent to do it. The connexion between the thought of an action and the will cannot be known *a priori*,

'. . . it has been shown, in treating of the understanding, that there is no connection of cause and effect, such as this is supposed to be, which is discoverable otherwise than by experience, and of which we can pretend to have any security by the simple consideration of the objects. All beings in the universe, considered in themselves, appear entirely loose and independent of each other. It is only by experience we learn their influence and connection.'[2] . . .

Both these arguments appear convincing; yet they are stated in so condensed a form that their precise value is by no means evident. In order to ascertain their full implications it is necessary to consider them in detail. Let us begin by considering the first argument and then see in what respect the second is connected with it; for, as we shall see, they are closely connected, if they are not merely a different expression of the same argument.

Now one of the things which Hume's first argument asserts

[1] *Treatise*, ii, p. 167.    [2] Ibid., p. 174.

is that passions, volitions, and actions being real entities cannot be true or false, self-evident or self-contradictory. It is true that in the passage quoted he refers to truth and falsehood generally, and not specifically to self-evidence and self-contradiction, but he has done so in an earlier passage.[1] Moreover, it is evident that self-evidence and self-contradiction are here included in the terms true and false, for, since Hume refers to both matters of fact and the relations between ideas, the truth and falsehood of which he speaks is both empirical and *a priori*. Now truth and falsehood, self-evidence and self-contradiction consist, Hume says, not in relations of ideas or in facts, but in agreement and disagreement to them. He does not specifically say what it is which, when true, agrees with real facts or relations, and, when false, disagrees with them, but it is clear that he is referring to propositions. His argument then is that truth and falsehood, self-evidence and self-contradiction are predicable only of propositions, and this in so far as the latter agree or disagree with the facts or relations of ideas which they assert; and, since actions, passions, and volitions are not propositions, but 'original facts and realities', it is meaningless to speak of them as either true or false.[1]

This argument is certainly valid; only propositions can be true or false, and passions, volitions, and actions are not propositions. My desire to go for a walk could not possibly be self-contradictory, any more than a tree or a horse could be self-contradictory. If anything were self-contradictory it would not be my desire to go for a walk, but the proposition which stated

[1] Hume advances the same argument in the section 'Of the Influencing Motives of the Will'. But his argument here is not so clear as in the later passage, which is perhaps the reason why he thought it necessary to state it a second time. The passage is none the less interesting. It refers only to passions and not to volitions and actions: 'A passion is an original existence, or, if you will, modification of existence, and contains not any representative quality, which renders it a copy of any other existence or modification. When I am angry, I am actually possessed with the passion, and in that emotion have no more a reference to any other object, than when I am thirsty, or sick, or more than five feet high. It is impossible, therefore, that this passion can be opposed by, or contradictory to truth and reason; since this contradiction consists in the disagreement of ideas, considered as copies, with those objects which they represent.' Ibid., p. 127.

that I had such a desire. Moreover, Hume here effectively
disposes of a part of the *a priori* argument, namely, in so far
as this argument is to be taken literally. Clarke and Wollaston
did indeed say that to will or to do certain acts is 'absurd' and
'contradictory'; moreover they attributed 'reason' to things;
the 'nature and reason of things' is a phrase met with in all
members of the *a priori* school, not excluding Malebranche.
Yet if this were the whole of Hume's argument it would be
altogether too simple. It disposes of Clarke's loose termino-
logy, and, in so far as this had its roots, not in mere carelessness,
but in a confusion of the laws of logic with the world of existents,
it disposes also of a genuine fallacy, but it does not on that
account destroy the whole substance of the *a priori* position.
Passions, volitions, and actions cannot be *self-contradictory* (it
is noteworthy that not even the most uncompromising of the
*a priori* moralists ever said they could be self-evident),[1] but it
does not follow from this that they cannot be *logically necessary*
or *logically impossible*. On the contrary, whenever we speak of
some proposition as self-contradictory, we are referring also
to a logically impossible state of affairs. When we say that the
proposition 'Deaf men can answer the telephone' or 'Triangles
have four sides' are self-contradictory, we imply that there are
no deaf men who can answer the telephone and that there are no
triangles with four sides, that their existence is logically impossible. Hence from the fact that passions, volitions, and
actions cannot be self-contradictory it does not follow that it
is nonsense to say that certain passions, volitions, and actions
are logically impossible and certain others logically necessary.

It may well be that the *a priori* school did not mean to say
that the willing and doing of some acts was self-contradictory,
but only that it was logically impossible. Clarke might have
agreed that properly speaking it is propositions which are self-
contradictory while the acts which such propositions are about
are logically impossible. Even so, he would probably have

---

[1] They say that the doing of some acts is self-contradictory, and they avoid
the absurdity of saying the doing of others is self-evident by arguing that the
*not* doing of them is self-contradictory.

thought that self-contradiction can be ascribed to propositions only in virtue of the fact that the state of affairs which they assert is itself logically impossible, whereas in fact the opposite is the case; we call that state of affairs impossible of which it is self-contradictory to assert that it exists. Thus, any member of the *a priori* school might have admitted that he was mistaken in predicating contradictoriness and absurdity of actions and volitions, and yet have maintained that certain actions and volitions can be logically impossible. 'It is logically impossible', he might say, 'to will unfitting acts, and it is self-contradictory to say that these acts can be willed.' There can be no doubt that some such view was at least part of what they had in mind. We must therefore inquire whether Hume's 'other considerations' contain anything which can be applied to the *a priori* doctrine in this modified form.

Now Hume advances two arguments which are to some extent concerned with this modified view. His first argument is that not only passions, volitions, and actions, but also propositions about them, are incapable of being self-contradictory or self-evident. For passions, volitions, and actions are single isolated facts, and no judgements about such facts can be demonstrable. 'Passions, volitions, and actions', Hume writes, '. . . [are] original facts and realities, complete in themselves, and *implying no reference to other passions, volitions, and actions.*'[1] And again, 'When I am angry, I am actually possessed with the passion, and in that emotion *have no more a reference to any other object*, than when I am thirsty, or sick, or more than five feet high.'[2] Since this is the case, judgements about passions, volitions, and actions cannot be self-contradictory or self-evident, for contradiction and self-evidence arise only when two or more ideas are compared. We are therefore no more justified in asserting that anybody must or must not have a certain passion, or volition, or that they must or must not do a certain action—that is in saying that actions, passions, and volitions are logically necessary or logically impossible—than we should be in saying that they are self-evident or self-contra-

---

[1] *Treatise*, ii, p. 167 (my italics).      [2] Ibid., p. 127 (my italics).

dictory. Hume's second argument is concerned with another aspect of this same problem. To say that we desire to do any action is another way of saying that we are moved by the thought of it. This is a causal proposition, and causal propositions, since they are a subclass of existential ones, and assert no more than a necessary succession in the order of existence, are also incapable of demonstration: 'All beings in the universe, *considered in themselves*, appear entirely loose and independent of each other.'[1] We can no more say that any single volition, passion, or action must or cannot come into existence as the result of the existence of something else, than we can say that they must or must not exist.

We must now consider these two arguments separately. Let us begin with the first. Hume's conclusion here rests on two premises. The first that propositions about passions, volitions, and actions are existential; the second that they are existential propositions of a special kind, ones which assert that a single fact exists or is given in experience without reference to any other. Hume, that is to say, seems to distinguish between propositions which are about one fact as related to another, and those which assert no more than that one isolated fact is the case: between 'there is a circle which is blue' and 'there is a circle' or 'there is a tree', and he maintains that propositions about passions, volitions, and actions are of the latter kind; they are simple factual statements of the form 'I am doing $x$', 'I will $x$', 'I desire $x$', and are in form like 'there is a tree'. It is for this reason that they are incapable of logical inconsistency, and hence cannot be either self-evident or self-contradictory.

Now Hume is evidently right in maintaining that propositions which do no more than assert that a certain fact is given in experience cannot be demonstrable; for existence and non-existence are no real predicates. To say of an object that it exists is not to add to our idea of this object anything which is capable either of being implied by this idea or of being incompatible with it. The predication of existence to any object

[1] *Treatise*, ii, p. 174 (my italics).

cannot qualify this object in such a way as to be implied by or to conflict with its other predicates.[1] Hence propositions which assert simply that an object exists or that it does not exist cannot be *a priori*. We cannot know *a priori* that a tree exists or that it does not exist, that *x* is angry or that *x* is pleased, for the propositions which assert these facts are in principle incapable of being either self-evident or self-contradictory.[2] Moreover, Hume is also right in stressing the point that it is because propositions about passions, volitions, and actions are about isolated facts and imply no reference to other passions, volitions, and actions that they are never capable of logical inconsistency. For propositions which are about the relations between facts are not existential but are of a form which allows of their being demonstrable. Propositions of the form 'there exists a circle' cannot be logically inconsistent, but the same argument does not apply to those of the form 'there exists a circle which is blue'. The view that existence is not a real predicate does not imply that propositions which assert that something exists and that it has more than one quality cannot be demonstrable. Existence, it is true, is not incompatible with any real quality, but yet it is incompatible with non-existence. The proposition 'there exists a red patch at point *s* at time *t*' is contradictory of the proposition 'there does not exist a red patch at point *s* at time *t*', and hence it is contradictory to all propositions which entail this second proposition, such as 'there exists a yellow patch at point *s* at time *t*'. Hence from the proposition that there does exist this red patch we can conclude *a priori* that there does not exist a yellow patch at the same time and place. Again we can say *a priori* that *if x* is the son of *y*, *y* must at some time have existed, but we cannot say *a priori* that *y* did at some time exist; though if we accept it as an empirical fact that *x* is the son of *y*, we can conclude by *a priori* reasoning, 'Since *x* is the son of *y*, *y* at some time existed.'[3]

[1] Ibid., i, p. 96: 'When I think of God, when I think of him as existent, and when I believe him to be existent, my idea of him neither increases nor diminishes.'     [2] See *Critique of Pure Reason*, A 598 ff.

[3] We must here note that the form of language which we use might lead us to believe that though there are no positive *a priori* existential propositions,

Now Hume is plainly right in applying this principle to passions, volitions, and actions in so far as propositions about them are about isolated events and not about any connexions between them. Moreover, it is to a considerable extent the case that propositions about them are about single events. The propositions 'I desire to do $x$', 'I will $x$', and 'I am doing $x$' do not refer to anything beyond the isolated existences which they assert. Hume is thus right when he says that it is 'not contrary to reason to prefer the destruction of the whole world to the scratching of my finger'; and 'It is not contrary to reason for me to choose my total ruin, to prevent the least uneasiness of an Indian, or person wholly unknown to me.'[1] On the other

yet there are negative ones; for it certainly seems that, though we cannot describe an object in such a way that its existence follows from our description, yet we can describe it in such a way that its non-existence follows from our description. Square circles and triangles with four sides cannot exist, and we feel tempted to say that being a square triangle is incompatible with existing. Yet if this were the case it would indeed be odd, for we should then be denying that saying that an object exists is a case of real predication, while maintaining that non-existence is a real predicate. But if we examine the cases where we feel tempted to say that the description of an object precludes its existence more carefully, we find that this temptation results merely from a linguistic trick. We are tempted to argue that 'square circles and triangles with four sides cannot exist' is true *a priori* because *existence* is incompatible with the natures of square-circular and triangular-four-sided figures. But in fact it is not existence which is incompatible with four-sided triangularity and circular squareness, but being square which is incompatible with being circular and being four-sided which is incompatible with being a triangle. We only come by this temptation because language allows us to say 'There is a square circle' or 'There is a triangle with four sides', and disguises the fact that in so doing we are asserting not one proposition but two, i.e. 'There exists a figure which is circular and which is also square' or 'There exists a figure which is a triangle and which has four sides'. These propositions are contradictory because '$x$ is circular' entails '$x$ is not square' which is contradictory to '$x$ is square', or '$x$ is a triangle' entails '$x$ has not four sides' which is contradictory to '$x$ has four sides'.

[1] *Treatise*, ii, p. 128. It may perhaps be thought that there is an exception to this rule. For it may be said that it is self-contradictory to assert that anybody did what is logically or physically impossible, or willed or desired what they thought to be physically or logically impossible. But it must be noticed that the impossibility of willing and desiring what is thought to be impossible is not generally accepted; it depends on the definition of willing and desiring and cannot be discussed here. But further, in saying that we cannot *do* the logically or physically impossible we are not referring to an isolated act. The case is exactly parallel to saying that there cannot be square circles. Just as it is not the case that there is anything about square circles which makes it impossible for them to be, but only something about squareness which makes it impossible for that which is square to be circular, so also there is nothing

hand, his argument is incomplete, for he overlooks the fact that although no single passion, volition, or action can be logically impossible, yet it may be impossible for certain passions, volitions, and actions to *coexist* with certain others. It is self-contradictory to say that at the same time I am both going to London and staying at home, and to say that I am willing or desiring both to stay and to go, and the facts which these propositions assert are logically incompatible. But though this oversight has for various reasons, which we will consider presently, considerable importance, yet it does not affect the main substance of his argument. For it remains the case that there are no simple *a priori* propositions about desiring, willing, and acting. Any demonstrative argument about these things must rest on at least one empirical premiss. It is demonstrative only in proceeding from its premisses by *a priori* reasoning.

Hume, as we have seen, elaborates his argument that propositions about desiring cannot be self-contradictory because they are existential by adding that they can also not be self-contradictory because, from another point of view, they are *causal*. The judgement 'I desire *x*' is existential in so far as it asserts the existence of a desire, but it is also causal in so far as what it asserts is that a feeling is aroused by the thought of doing *x*. Saying that *x* is the cause of *y*, equally with saying that *x* exists, is not saying anything which is implied by or is incompatible with its being *x*. Hence it cannot be self-contradictory to say that one event is caused by another; it would not be self-contradictory to say that heat causes ice or that sand-storms cause camels, and, in the present case, it would not be self-contradictory to say that the thought of any action causes or fails to cause me to feel moved to do it. Yet here again we must add that, granted an empirical premiss, certain

about either the logically or the physically impossible which makes it impossible to be done. It is not the case that we cannot draw square circles because square circles are not the kind of thing which can be drawn, nor is it the case that we cannot fly to the moon because flying to the moon is not the sort of thing which can be done. It is only the case that we can draw no object which is square and circular, because no object can possess both these qualities, and that it cannot be true both that flying to the moon is physically impossible and that *x* has flown there.

other causal propositions can follow *a priori*. Thus, given that heat causes water to boil and that electricity in certain conditions is heat, it follows *a priori* that electricity in these conditions will cause water to boil.

Now these arguments together are on the whole an adequate answer to the *a priori* school. Clarke and his followers certainly maintained not that some passions, volitions, and actions were the necessary consequence of others, or were necessarily precluded by them, but that they were necessary or impossible in themselves alone. They did not argue that *given* the premises '*x* wills to do fitting acts', and '*x* knows *y* to be fitting', it is demonstrably certain that he must will *y*, but that there is an absolute *a priori* necessity of willing fitting acts.[1] Hume's answer to this argument and to all others of like form is completely satisfactory. He shows that it is wholly illegitimate to assert as demonstrably certain that any action must be willed or desired, unless some other judgement about willing and desiring which is not *a priori* is already accepted.

Yet there remains one point to be considered. For, as we have already remarked, Hume's argument as it stands is concerned with a wider problem than that of the demonstrability of proper *practical* judgements. Even Clarke was implicitly more concerned with the question whether certain passions, volitions, and actions are logically impossible, than with whether they are 'morally' impossible, that is, whether it is impossible *knowingly* to will certain acts. And this is the all-important question for the influence of reason on action, for

---

[1] This is of course not true of Hobbes, who argued that the breaking of promises is self-contradictory (see above, Ch. I, p. 9). Hobbes argued that in making a promise we were in fact willing to do a certain act, and that in breaking it we were willing not to do it. If breaking promises consisted as he thought in willing and not willing the same act at the same time, Hobbes would certainly be right in saying that it is not possible to break promises. Clearly he is wrong; in so far as promises are lying promises, no act has been willed, and in so far as they are genuine promises which are broken what is willed at one time is not willed at another. Moreover, it seems doubtful if we can say that the making of a promise is actually the willing of an act, for clearly there is a difference between willing and resolving. But in any case the whole argument is exceedingly odd, for if it were true it would prove that promises could never be broken.

as we have pointed out, judgements which are simply about the logical impossibility of passions, volitions, and actions cannot affect action at all; if it is impossible to do, will, or desire *y*, it follows that in no circumstances will *y* be done, willed, or desired, and our knowledge of this impossibility will not be able to affect us. The question is whether it is possible to judge *a priori* that a certain action must be or cannot be willed, desired, or done on reflection. That such judgements are possible seems to have been the underlying contention of the *a priori* school; for if they had meant to say no more than that certain actions, desires, and volitions were literally impossible, they would have been quite unable to make these *a priori* judgements the basis of morality; it would then have followed that immoral action is logically impossible.

Hume does not explicitly discuss this point, but it is evident that his answer to it is included in the more general argument which we have considered. Now in order to show how his more general argument can be applied to this case, it is not necessary to speak separately about desiring, willing, and acting. For it is plain that if anything can influence our doing and willing on reflection which does not influence it without reflection, it must be some cause which becomes operative only as the result of a rational process. And since, according to Hume, the only causes of willing and acting are motives or desires which determine us to do one thing rather than another, it follows that the problem of practical judgements is confined to the question whether reflection is capable of introducing new motives to action and of eliminating existing ones. There can be no doubt that Hume saw the problem in this light, for his whole discussion of the influence of *a priori* reasoning is a discussion of the question: 'Can reason alone be the *motive* to any action of the will'? The question: 'Are demonstrative practical judgements possible' is, therefore, synonymous with the question: 'Are there any *a priori* judgements about the necessity of having a certain motive on reflection': i.e. judgements about the necessity of being moved on reflection to do one thing rather than another. Both Hume's arguments can evidently be applied to this problem, but of the two it is the *causal* argument which can be applied most directly. We could apply the first by saying that from the fact that we cannot say *a priori* that any single desire must exist, it follows that we cannot say *a priori* that any single desire must exist on reflection. But the second argument has a clearer application. This argument is that we cannot say *a priori* that the thought of any action must move us to do the action, and from this it follows that we cannot say *a priori* that the thought of any action must move us on reflection. For to be moved on reflection is to be affected by an idea, which was not previously before the mind, or at least was not before the mind in an articulate form, or was not before the mind to the exclusion of others. Saying that an idea will affect us when it is adequately considered, equally with saying that it affects us now, is asserting a causal proposition about the effect of an idea.

We can conclude that Hume has shown that there can be no *a priori* propositions about the necessity of being moved by the thought of any single thing. There are no *a priori* propositions which assert that on reflection $x$ must be moved to do $y$, for all such propositions are based on empirical premises about $x$'s other desires. This is a fact which Hume re-emphasizes again and again; 'Even in human nature', he says, 'no relation can ever alone produce any action.'[1] Moreover, it is this argument which, by implication, establishes Hume's point that moral judgements, if there are any, cannot be *a priori*, a conclusion which he draws in no ambiguous terms:

'Since morals . . . have an influence on the actions and affections, it follows that they cannot be derived from reason; and that because reason *alone* . . . can never have any such influence. Morals excite passions, and produce or prevent actions. Reason *of itself* is utterly impotent in this particular.'[2]

Such then was Hume's answer to the theory which he

---

[1] *Treatise*, ii, p. 174.
[2] Ibid., p. 167 (my italics). It is clear from the qualification of 'reason' in this passage by 'of itself' and 'alone' that Hume is here referring to *a priori* reason. Empirical reason is never reason 'alone'. The conclusions of empirical reasoning always require the use of the senses.

describes as the theory that 'morality like truth can be discerned merely by ideas, their juxtaposition and comparison'. Hume's conclusion here follows from the three premisses that moral judgements must be practical, that in order to be practical a judgement must be about a relation between the thought of an action and the agent's will, and that judgements about this relation being causal can never be *a priori*.[1]

Hume's argument then succeeds in showing that there are no practical *a priori* judgements, no judgements, that is to say, which are established by demonstrative reasoning alone, but he ignores altogether the question whether there are practical judgements which can be deduced by demonstrative reasoning from empirical premisses. It is true indeed that in the context of refuting the Clarkians the answer to this question was irrelevant, but in relation to the problem of reason and conduct as a whole it is of the utmost importance. We must therefore, in conclusion, say something about it, in order that we may be able to assess the value of Hume's arguments as a whole.

There are, I think, five types of case where we can draw demonstrative practical conclusions from empirical premisses. There may well be more, but these will at least suffice as examples. Let us begin by enumerating them:

(i) If I desire to do a *member* of a *class* of acts *x*, and then judge that an act *y* is a member of this class, then, if I contemplate these two facts together, I can conclude *a priori* that (as long as I continue to desire to do a member of the class *x*) I must desire *y*. (ii) If I desire to do an act which belongs to a *species* of a *genus* of acts *x*, and then judge that *y* belongs to a species of this genus *x*, then, if I contemplate these two facts together, I can conclude *a priori* that (as long as I continue to desire to do an act which belongs to a species of a genus *x*) I must desire *y*. (iii) If I desire to do an act *x* which is a *process* and then judge that *y* is a *constituent* of this process, then, on contemplating these two facts together, I can conclude *a priori* that (as long as I continue to desire *x*) I must desire *y*. (iv) If I desire

---

[1] See the passage quoted above, p. 51.

to do an act *x*, and then judge that doing *x* has a *material impli-cation y*, I can, on contemplating these two facts together, conclude *a priori* that (as long as I continue to desire *x*) I must desire *y*.[1]    (v) If, when I consider them separately, I desire to do both of two acts *x* and *y*, and then judge that the doing of *x* is *incompatible* with the doing of *y*, then, if I contemplate these two facts together, I can conclude *a priori* that I must desire to do either *x* or *y* but cannot desire both.

It will not be necessary to consider all these cases separately in the same detail. The first four cases are susceptible to very similar analysis, and we may take that of *class-member* as an example.

The question with which we are concerned is why in these cases the judgement that I must desire *y* is both *demonstrable* and *practical*. Now, to say that I desire to do an act which is a member of the class *x* is to say that the idea of doing an act which is a member of this class moves me to do it, e.g. that I am moved by the thought of 'riding a horse'. I then judge that an act *y is* a member of the class of acts *x*; e.g. that 'riding this' or 'riding Black Bess' is 'riding a horse'; and, if I contem-plate these two facts (i.e. that I desire to ride a horse and riding Black Bess is riding a horse), I will *necessarily* come into a state of desiring to ride Black Bess. For I cannot be moved by the thought of a member of the class *x* and think that *y is* a member of the class *x* without being moved by the thought of *y*, and in judging that 'riding Black Bess' *is* 'riding a horse', I *am* judging that *y is* a member of the class *x*. Hence it is that

---

[1] It will be noticed that in all four cases we have introduced the qualifying phrase 'so long as I continue to desire an act of the genus *x*, or a member of the class *x*, or *x'*. This qualification is introduced because in fact it may always be the case that when I have assented to the minor premiss I shall abandon my desire for an act of the genus *x*, a member of the class *x*, or *x*, rather than come to desire *y*. For the minor premiss, since it always tells me something about either the relational or intrinsic nature of acts of the genus *x*, or class *x*, or *x*, may, by altering my idea of this thing, change my desire into indifference or aversion. If I desire to do an act which is a member of the class 'riding horses', I may judge that riding Black Bess is riding a horse and yet not be moved to ride Black Bess, because riding *Black Bess* would not merely have the charac-teristic of belonging to the class of acts 'riding a horse' but a variety of other characteristics as well. As the result of this judgement my desire to ride *a* horse may be modified.

I must conclude that 'riding Black Bess' is what I must desire on contemplation, and this conclusion follows analytically from the premiss asserting my desire for a member of the class $x$ *together with* the premiss that I judge $y$ to be a member of this class.

Now, it will I think be readily admitted that this judgement is demonstrable, that it follows analytically from the given premisses, but perhaps it will be argued that though demonstrable it is not practical. The judgement, it will be said, is after all analytic precisely because my desire to ride Black Bess is already included in my desire to ride a horse. My desire for *a* member of a class is *already* a desire for whatever happens to be such a member. How then can this judgement be practical? How is it that it can bring me into a *new* state of desiring, for surely the judgement is only analytic because it is no more than a new way of asserting an already premissed desire? My desire to ride *a* horse *is* a desire to ride Black Bess, so evidently the judgement, 'Since I desire to ride a horse and Black Bess is a horse I must desire to ride Black Bess' cannot affect me at all. But this is a spurious argument. In the first place, we have to notice that my desire to do an act which is a member of a class $x$ is not a desire to do $y$ which is a member of this class, unless $y$ is *recognized* by me to be such a member. My desire to ride a horse is not a desire to ride Black Bess unless I *know* or *think* that Black Bess is a horse—and if I do this it *is* a desire to ride Black Bess whether I am right in thinking that Black Bess is a horse or not. Hence it does not in any case follow from the premisses 'I desire to ride a horse' and 'Black Bess *is* a horse' that I am already desiring to ride Black Bess. But secondly, even when I do know or think that Black Bess is a horse, my desire to ride *a* horse will not *be* a desire to ride Black Bess until I am aware *both* of the fact that I desire to ride a horse *and* that Black Bess is a horse. That is to say, my desire to ride a horse and my judgement or opinion that Black Bess is a horse, must be before my mind *simultaneously*. I should still not desire to ride Black Bess if I first thought of my desire to ride *a* horse, and only afterwards of the fact that Black Bess was a horse. For it is only when I realize the identity of the kind of thing which I desire and the kind of thing which riding Black Bess is that I come to be aware of my desire for the one *as* a desire for the other. I cannot realize this identity as long as I think of the major and the minor premisses successively. I can only do so if I think of them jointly. Hence, in order to give rise to a desire to ride Black Bess, the two facts, that I desire to ride a horse and that Black Bess is a horse, must be synthesized in my consciousness. I admit that on certain occasions this synthesis may take place without judgement. The two facts may just happen to present themselves simultaneously before my mind and may result in my desire to ride Black Bess, without my ever co-contemplating them intentionally and without my drawing a conclusion from them in the form of a judgement. But although synthesis may occur in this way, it is evidently not the only way in which it occurs. I may also bring the two facts before my mind intentionally and with a view to finding out what conclusions can be drawn from them. In this case, I ask myself what I must desire to do in view of the fact that I desire to ride a horse and think that Black Bess is a horse, and, from the synthesizing of these two facts which I thus bring about, there emerges simultaneously a desire to ride Black Bess and a demonstrative practical judgement that, in view of these facts, Black Bess is what I must desire to ride. It is the process of *judging* which here causes this desire, the process which concludes in both a judgement and a desire. It follows that the judgement 'Since I desire a member of the class $x$ and $y$ is a member of the class $x$ I must desire $y$' is analytic and practical, although the state of desire to which the judgement gives rise may sometimes be caused without it.

About our *second* type of demonstrative practical judgements little need be said. They are demonstrative and practical for the same reasons as those of the class-member type. There are, however, certain differences which we may note in passing. The demonstrative practical judgements of the genus-species type differ from those of the class-member type in that both the minor premiss and the major are concerned with universals. The major premiss asserts, for instance, 'I desire to ride an animal', and the minor 'riding a horse is riding an animal'. The conclusion also, therefore, concerns a universal; it is of the form 'I must desire to ride a horse'. It follows from this that, although judgements of this type are practical in that they cause desire, for the agent comes into a state of desiring to ride a horse, yet what they cause is only a desire for something of universal description. Before this desire can actually issue in action it will be necessary for me to make a further judgement, and this of the class-member type, e.g. that Black Bess is a horse, and that, therefore, I must want to ride Black Bess.[1]

In cases of this type, as indeed in all the others also, the major premiss is always empirical. But here I think it is true to say that the minor may be either empirical or *a priori*. It is certainly *a priori* when it asserts that first paying a man £100 and then paying him £50 is a species of paying him £150. Perhaps it is *a priori* also when it asserts that 'riding a horse is riding an animal', but it would be empirical if it asserted that 'going out in the rain is getting wet'.

Our *third* type of judgement differs from these two in that here both the major and the minor premiss may refer either to

---

[1] This point is made by Aristotle, *Eth. Nic.*, Book VI, 1141b (see W. D. Ross's translation): 'Nor is practical wisdom concerned with universals only—it must also recognize the particulars. . . . This is why some who do not know, and especially those who have experience, are more practical than others who know; for if a man knew that light meats are digestible and wholesome, but did not know which sorts of meat are light, he would not produce health, but the man who knows that chicken is wholesome is more likely to produce health.' We must note, however, that here Aristotle does not carry his example quite far enough, for the judgement that 'chicken is light meat' is itself about a genus-species relation. Chicken is itself a universal. We still do not know what things are chickens. However, Aristotle makes the same point again later on, and this time he does insist on knowledge of genuine particulars. See 1147a: 'Further, since there are two kinds of premisses, there is nothing to prevent a man's having both premisses and acting against his knowledge, provided he is using only the universal premiss and not the particular; for it is particular acts that have to be done. And there are also two kinds of universal term; one is predicable of the agent, the other of the object; e.g., "dry food is good for everyman", and "I am a man", or "such and such a food is dry"; but whether "this food is such and such", of this the incontinent man either has not or is not exercising the knowledge.'

universals or to particulars, provided only that both refer to the same. Thus the major may assert that I desire a process of universal description, such as going on a sea voyage, and the minor 'sleeping in bunks or hammocks are constituents of such journeys'. Or the major that I desire to go to London on the 10.20 this morning, and the minor that mounting this train and standing in the corridor are constituents of this journey. In this case also the minor may be either empirical or *a priori*.

The *fourth* type of judgement is like the third, and raises no new problems. Thus the major may be that I desire to go rock-climbing, and the minor that rock-climbing materially implies buying a pair of nailed boots. Or the major that I desire to climb on Idwal Slabs this morning, and the minor that climbing on Idwal Slabs this morning materially implies bringing my rope.

The *fifth* type of judgement is rather different from the other four. It is perhaps not easy to see why in this case the conclusion does follow analytically from the premisses. It will be necessary therefore to consider it at greater length. We have said that when, on considering $x$ and $y$ separately, I desire each *and* judge that $x$ is incompatible with $y$, then I shall conclude that I must desire either $x$ or $y$, but cannot desire both. This judgement is demonstrable because, when on considering $x$ and $y$ separately I am moved by the thought of each, the thought of each alone is the cause of my being moved, but when I consider them together I judge that the doing of $x$ is equivalent to the not doing of $y$ and the doing of $y$ equivalent to the not doing of $x$;[1] and from this it follows *a priori* that if I consider the minor premiss alone, I cannot be moved to do both $x$ and $y$ at the same time, for while I am thinking that $x$ is incompatible with $y$, my being moved to do $x$ is also my not being moved to do $y$, and my being moved to do $y$ is also my not being moved to do $x$. But if I consider the minor premiss

---

[1] In this case also the minor premiss may be either *a priori* or empirical. It would be *a priori* if I judged, for instance, that going to London at 10 o'clock on Wednesday the 16th of June 1945 is incompatible with going to Birmingham at the same time. It would be empirical if I judged that going shopping this afternoon is incompatible with being home in time for tea.

together with the major, i.e. together with the fact that, when I consider them separately, I want to do $x$ and $y$, then I must as the result of this consideration be moved to do *either x or y*; for each considered singly is the cause of my being moved, and their incompatibility considered together with this fact must result in my being moved to do either the one or the other. Let us consider an example. When I consider the possibility of spending the whole of the long vacation in the Dolomites, I am moved by the thought of doing so. When I consider the possibility of spending the whole of the long vacation on an Arctic expedition, I am moved by this thought also. I then judge that it is impossible for me both to spend the whole of the long vacation climbing in the Dolomites and the whole of the long vacation on an Arctic expedition. In so far as I consider this fact it is impossible for me to be moved both by the thought of going to the Dolomites and by the thought of going on the Arctic expedition, for my idea of going to the Dolomites is then also an idea of not going to the Arctic, and my idea of going to the Arctic an idea of not going to the Dolomites. But, in so far as I consider this fact together with the fact that, when I entertained these two ideas separately, each had moving force, I must be moved *either* to spend the whole of the long vacation in the Dolomites *or* to spend the whole of the long vacation in the Arctic. That is to say, I must *choose* between the two. For just as I cannot desire both together, so also I cannot abandon my desire for either as long as I still desire each separately. Here again we must observe that it is not the *fact* that doing $y$ is incompatible with doing $z$, which makes it impossible to desire both on reflection, but the *judgement* that they are incompatible.

In considering the nature of all these judgements it must be kept in mind that in each case the subject is 'I'. If this were not so, the judgements, though still analytic, would not be practical. For in order for a judgement to be practical it must be made by the person who is himself the subject of it. The judgement '*You* must on reflection be moved by the thought of $x$, since you desire to do a thing of the kind $y$ and judge $x$

to be a thing of the kind $y$', is not practical, although it may well influence an agent by inducing him to make such a judgement for himself, i.e. a judgement where 'I' is substituted for 'you'.

In conclusion, there is one more point to be considered. It may seem surprising that our list of demonstrative practical judgements inferred from empirical premisses has not included judgements about *means to ends*. It is commonly assumed that he who desires the end must desire the means also (or else cease to desire the end), and this, it is thought, is true *a priori*. Hence, might we not add to our list a *sixth* type of judgement, i.e. judgements whereby from the premisses 'I desire $x$' and 'I judge $y$ to be a means to $x$', I conclude *a priori* that I must desire $y$? Now I do indeed think that such a conclusion follows analytically from its premisses, but this does not justify us in regarding these judgements as a distinct type. In fact it seems that what are commonly regarded as judgements about the necessity of adopting the means to a desired end are not a distinct type of practical judgement at all, for what is commonly meant by being a means to an end is neither a single nor a unique relation, but merely a number of special cases of the relations involved in the practical judgements we have already discussed.

There seem to be four kinds of judgements, all instances of types we have considered above, which are normally regarded as judgements about means to ends. This point is best illustrated by considering examples. (i) the judgement 'In order to climb Idwal Slabs I must first walk to Cwm Idwal' would normally be regarded as a judgement about a means to an end. Now, clearly, this is a judgement about a *material implication*. To judge that 'Since I desire to climb Idwal Slabs and I judge that in order to do this I must walk to Cwm Idwal, I must, on contemplating these two facts together, desire to walk to Cwm Idwal' is to make a judgement of our fourth type.[1] (Of

---

[1] This seems to be the kind of means-ends practical judgement discussed by Kant and considered by him as analytic. See 'The Fundamental Principles of the Metaphysics of Morals' in Abbott's *Kant's Theory of Ethics*, p. 34: 'Whoever wills the end, wills also (so far as reason decides his conduct) the means in his power which are indispensably necessary thereto. This proposition

course it does not follow that all judgements of type four can be regarded as means-ends judgements. They can only be so regarded where the relation of material implication holds between a desired *act* or *state* and one of its *necessary prerequisites*.) Now it is, I think, judgements of this kind which we most commonly have in mind when we speak about means-ends judgements, and there are good reasons for thinking that the term 'means-ends' should properly be restricted to such judgements. On the other hand, there can be no doubt that we do in fact use this term more widely. Thus (ii) the judgement 'In order to climb Idwal Slabs I must use my hands' would also normally be regarded as a means-ends judgement. This clearly is not the same type of judgement as 'In order to climb Idwal Slabs I must walk to Cwm Idwal', for it is not a judgement about one act being *materially implied* by another but about one act being *contained within* another. Using my hands is one of the things of which the complex process 'climbing Idwal Slabs' is made up. It is, therefore, numbered not among the relational but among the intrinsic characteristics of this act. Hence the practical judgement 'Since I desire to climb Idwal Slabs and judge that in order to climb Idwal Slabs I must use my hands, I must, on contemplating these two facts together, desire to use my hands' is a judgement of the *process-constituent* type. Again (iii) the judgement 'In order to climb the Holly Tree Wall I must climb by a "severe" route' would be regarded as a means-ends judgement. But this judgement is neither about a material implication of climbing up Holly Tree Wall

is, as regards the volition, analytical; for, in willing an object as my effect, there is already thought the causality of myself as an acting cause, that is to say, the use of the means; and the imperative educes from the conception of the volition of an end the conception of actions necessary to this end. Synthetical propositions must no doubt be employed in defining the means to a proposed end; but they do not concern the principle, the act of the will, but the object and its realization. Ex. gr., that in order to bisect a line on an unerring principle I must draw from its extremities two intersecting arcs; this no doubt is taught by mathematics only by synthetical propositions; but if I know that it is only by this process that the intended operation can be performed, then to say that if I fully will the operation, I will also the action required for it, is an analytical proposition; for it is one and the same thing to conceive something as an effect which I can produce in a certain way, and to conceive myself as acting in this way.'

nor about a constituent of this climb. The act of climbing Holly Tree Wall is a *genus* with different *species* and 'climbing a "severe"' is one of these. Finally (iv) the judgement 'In order to climb up a "severe" on Holly Tree Wall I must climb up Javelin Gully' would also be regarded as a judgement about a means to an end, but this is a judgement about a *class-membership*; 'climbing up Javelin Gully' is a member of the class of acts 'climbing up a "severe" on Holly Tree Wall'.

Hence we see that what are commonly called practical means-ends judgements do not constitute a special type of demonstrative practical judgement but are simply special cases of a variety of types of such judgement each with a more general form. There is no difficulty in understanding why certain material implication judgements should warrant the special title 'judgements about means to ends'. For some of these judgements assert that the doing of one action is a necessary prerequisite to the doing of another. They refer to a special case of material implication, and this, together with the pragmatic significance of this special case, entitles them to a separate name. But it is not equally evident why certain judgements of the other three types are also called judgements about means to ends, nor what it is which distinguishes these judgements from others of their kind which are not so called. We can call one action a means to another when it is a necessary prerequisite of this other; but it is, strictly speaking, improper to refer to a constituent as the necessary prerequisite of a process, or to an act which is a species of a genus, or a member of a class, as a necessary prerequisite of an act which belongs to a species of this genus or which is a member of this class. For to say that something is a necessary prerequisite is to refer to one thing as necessarily preceding another in *time*. But when we say that we cannot enact a process $x$ without doing $y$ which is one of its constituents, or do an act which belongs to a species of a genus $x$ without doing $y$ which does belong to a species of this genus, or do an act which is a member of a class without doing $y$ which is a member of this class, we are not referring to any order in the time sequence of events. Nor are the relations which we refer to in these cases relations between one act and another, for in none is the so-called 'means' anything *separate* from the end. In the process-constituent case the 'means' is an integral part of the desired end, and in the genus-species and class-member cases the 'means' is no more than a particular description of the end. It is true that in all four cases we can say that we must do *y in order to* do *x*, but the use of 'in order to' conceals an important difference between 'necessary connexion' in the *temporal* and in the *logical* order. Hence there are good reasons for thinking that the wide popular application of 'means-ends' is an improper one.

We have now seen that there are certain demonstrable practical judgements which rest on empirical premisses. These judgements Hume ignores altogether. In his general argument he assumes that judgements about desires or their causes are always about single facts or single causal relations, and it is this false assumption which leads him to neglect the judgements which we have just considered. In fact he does not merely overlook them; sometimes he even goes so far as to deny them, at least by implication. We have already noted Hume's illustration of his point that desires cannot be called unreasonable *a priori*: 'It is not contrary to reason for me to prefer the destruction of the whole world to the scratching of my finger. It is not contrary to reason for me to choose my total ruin to prevent the least uneasiness of an Indian or person wholly unknown to me.'[1] With this argument we have agreed. No single desire can itself be contrary to reason, and a preference for one thing rather than another is a single desire. But to these examples Hume adds another: 'It is as little contrary to reason to prefer even my own *acknowledged* lesser good to my greater, and have a more ardent affection for the former than the latter.'[1] Now, it is true, of course, that I may not desire good at all. But this is not the case that Hume is thinking of. For he accepts it as a very well-founded empirical fact that men do desire good; he thinks in fact that the

---

[1] *Treatise*, ii, p. 128 (my italics).

great majority of acts are desired in proportion to the good which is expected from them.[1] And here he is clearly thinking of the case not where good is not desired at all, but where good itself is desired and the instance of good is not. He is thinking, for example, of the case where I shall incur greater good by remaining sober than by getting drunk, and yet desire to get drunk. But evidently Hume's argument is fallacious, for granted the premiss which he seems to accept, i.e. that we have a desire for 'whatever is an instance of good', then we have here a case of the first type of judgement which we have discussed. If I desire what is conducive to my good, and judge that remaining sober will be conducive to my good, then, in so far as I am aware of these two facts simultaneously, or 'acknowledge' them, I must desire to remain sober. The case is only slightly complicated by Hume's introduction of 'preference', but it is not in principle any different on this account. For to say that I desire to do an act which is an instance of that which will conduce to my good is not any different from saying 'I desire to do that act which will conduce *most* to my good'. If I desire to do an act solely on account of its goodness, I must desire to do that which has the greater quantity of goodness. I cannot, therefore, prefer my own lesser to my greater good, while *at the same time acknowledging* it as my lesser good. Hume's remark would only have been true if he had omitted the word 'acknowledged'.[2]

[1] *Treatise*, ii, p. 148.

[2] It would be fruitless to speculate at length about the reasons why Hume overlooked these judgements, yet there is one ground on which his omission may well be accounted for. We have argued that in each case the practical judgement is demonstrable because it is impossible to conceive of $y$ as implied by or an instance of $x$ and *at the same time* be affected by $y$ in a manner different from that in which we are affected by $x$. But this argument evidently presupposes an identity of the self which is at the same time aware of the relation between $x$ and $y$ and is affected by $x$. It presupposes that the awareness of being affected by $x$ is precisely *contemporary* with the awareness of the relation between $x$ and $y$. On Hume's view of the self, the subject which is affected by the thought of $x$ is not identical with that which judges about this relation, for according to him, the awareness of being affected by $x$, and the awareness of its relation to $y$ cannot be strictly contemporary. Hume regards the self as composed of a series of perceptions which are strictly *successive* in time. It follows that on his view of the self there would be no judgements of the kind which we have described; for the awareness of the minor premiss would never be contem-

Thus Hume overlooked, or even denied, the possibility of the practical demonstrative judgements based on empirical premisses, but it must be admitted that these judgements are of the greatest importance. They play a prominent part in the determination of our conduct, and without them the theoretical judgements which we discussed at the beginning of this chapter might fail to take effect. A man may desire to pay £50 plus £100, and he may judge that £50 plus £100 amounts to £150, but he may still not come to desire to pay £150. In order for this judgement to awaken a desire for the latter it is necessary that he should be simultaneously aware of his former desire and of this judgement. Without the simultaneous awareness of both desire and judgement the awareness of each will remain totally dissociated, and, so long as they remain dissociated, it is impossible for them to have the effect which would result from the contemporaneous awareness of both. We cannot draw any conclusions from two separate premisses which are not the objects of the same consciousness; until they are combined they remain in what we might call logic-tight compartments. This is true of the case where premisses considered jointly would give rise to purely theoretical conclusions as well as of that where they arouse desires. A man may accept the premiss 'All men who die for their country are honourable'. He may further judge '$X$, who is a Hottentot, died for his country', but he may deny that '$X$ is honourable'. We may fail to convince him that if these two premisses are true, $X$ must be honourable, because his awareness that all men who die for their country are honourable may never be *strictly contemporary* with his awareness that $X$ died for his country. In this case we shall say that he is stupid or unreasonable; and we then mean that he is unable to review simultaneously the different propositions which he believes to be true; in fact that he is incapable of thinking

porary with the awareness of the major. But on Hume's view of the self as consisting of successive perceptions, many other views which he does not hesitate to advance would be logically excluded, e.g. his analysis of the artificial virtues. In fact it is very doubtful whether, if our perceptions are always successive, it is possible to make any judgements at all, for it seems that all judging involves synthesis.

or synthesizing. In all cases where it is possible to draw from two premisses a conclusion which we could not draw from either considered in itself, or to be affected by two judgements in a way in which we should not be affected by either separately, it is necessary that these two premisses should be synthesized in consciousness. Our making of this synthesis in practical matters is promoted by practical inquiry and practical judgement. It is in practical inquiry that we set out to discover the connexions between our already existing desires and that which is implied by them, or is an instance of them. And it is in the practical judgement that we draw the conclusions from the premisses which we have discovered and thereby modify our conduct.

# CHAPTER IV

# EMPIRICAL REASON AND CONDUCT

AS yet we have considered only Hume's account of the influence on action of *a priori* judgements; we have still to see what he has to say about the influence of empirical ones. It is here that his contributions to our problem appear in their most positive and suggestive form.

In the last chapter we distinguished between the practical influence of what we have called *theoretical* and what we have called *practical* judgements: judgements, that is to say, whose practical influence is merely incidental and those whose influence is essential. We concluded there that Hume allowed that theoretical *a priori* judgements can have practical influence, but that he denied the possibility of *practical a priori* judgements. In this chapter also it will be convenient to divide our discussion into two parts, and to consider theoretical and practical empirical judgements separately. But in doing so we must again call attention to the fact that, although the division of influencing judgements into these two kinds is implicit in the *Treatise*, it is certainly not explicit, and, in so arranging our argument, we are not attributing to Hume any hard-and-fast division of judgements into these two kinds.

Let us begin by considering Hume's analysis of those empirical judgements which influence action but are also theoretical. His remarks about these judgements are far more elaborate than those about their *a priori* counterparts. In considering the latter he did not go beyond admitting that 'mathematics, indeed, are useful in all mechanical operations, and arithmetic in almost every art and profession',[1] while at the same time arguing that such judgements do not have influence 'of themselves', and illustrating this point with the single example of the merchant who wished to pay his debts, and was affected by his calculations of their total.[2] There we were forced to reconstruct the detail of this influence for ourselves.

---

[1] *Treatise*, ii, p. 126.    [2] See above, Chapter III.

But his account of the influence of theoretical empirical judgements is more elaborate. It is, in fact, the structure of his argument here which confirms our previous interpretation.

Hume's first statement of this argument occurs in the section 'Of the Influencing Motives of the Will', but it is repeated in somewhat greater detail in the section 'Moral Distinctions not Derived from Reason'. In the first of these sections Hume writes:

'. . . it is only in two senses that any affection can be called unreasonable. First, When a passion, such as hope or fear, grief or joy, despair or security, is founded on the supposition of the existence of objects, which do not really exist. Secondly, When in exerting any passion in action, we choose a means insufficient for the designed end, and deceive ourselves in our judgement of causes and effects.'[1]

And in the second:

'. . . reason, in a strict and philosophical sense, can have an influence on our conduct only after two ways: either when it excites a passion, by informing us of the existence of something which is a proper object of it; or when it discovers the connection of causes and effects, so as to afford us means of exerting any passion. These are the only kinds of judgements which can accompany our actions, or can be said to produce them in any manner; and it must be allowed, that these judgements may often be false and erroneous. A person may be affected with passion, by supposing a pain or pleasure to lie in an object which has no tendency to produce either of these sensations, or which produces the contrary to what is imagined. A person may also take false measures for the attaining of his end, and may retard, by his foolish conduct, instead of forwarding the execution of any object.'[2]

Hume argues here that there are two kinds of empirical judgement which can influence action: judgements about means to ends and judgements about the nature and existence of objects. When I judge that 'If I take the 10.20 I shall be in London by 12 o'clock', I make a judgement which can affect my behaviour towards the 10.20; when I judge that 'This apple is sweet', I make a judgement which can affect my behaviour towards this apple. For, if I desire to be in London by 12 o'clock, the judgement 'If I go on the 10.20 I shall be in London by 12

---

[1] *Treatise*, ii, p. 127.          [2] Ibid., p. 168.

o'clock' may raise in me a desire to travel by this train; and, if I desire to eat a sweet apple, the judgement 'This apple is sweet' may raise in me a desire to eat 'this apple'. Hume calls such judgements the 'oblique' or 'mediate' causes of action, for, like those which we discussed in the last chapter, 'it is not in themselves that they have influence'. What causes action immediately is *desire*, and these judgements are only effective if, and in so far as, they bring to our attention certain facts which can affect our desires. When our actions are affected by *true* judgements of these kinds we can, though in an 'improper sense', say that they are *reasonable*; and when they are affected by *false* ones we can say that they are *unreasonable*. My action in taking the 10.20 will be reasonable if I want to be in London by 12 o'clock, and if my judgement that this train arrives there by that time is true; it will be unreasonable if this judgement is false.

It is evident that this view of determination of conduct by empirical judgements has great prima-facie plausibility. Little introspection will suffice to show that our passions and actions are often affected in this way. Moreover, frequently it is by communicating these judgements that we try to influence the conduct of others. We urge them to do some acts by pointing out their possibility, nature, or consequences; 'Have an apple', we suggest, and we add, as an incentive, 'It is nice and sweet'. Or we deter somebody from eating an apple by the mere remark 'That's sour'. We cause or prevent people from getting on trains simply by saying, 'This is the train which goes to Paddington' and 'That one doesn't go beyond Reading'. In short, granted a desire to go to London, or to eat a ripe apple, the judgements which indicate *how* to go to London and *what* apples are ripe will affect our conduct. That these judgements have such an effect is a common datum of experience. Yet the analysis of how they have it is complex and is different in the two cases. It is to this analysis that we must now turn.

Let us begin by considering judgements about means to ends. Hume describes these as 'directing' judgements.[1] They

------

[1] Ibid., p. 171.

are judgements which *direct passions*, and they depend for their effect on the prior existence of these passions. The judgement '*x* is a means to *y*' can never give rise to a desire to do *x* unless *y* is already desired. When we desire an end, Hume argues, 'reasoning takes place to discover' the means to this end, and 'according as our reasoning varies, our actions receive a subsequent variation'. But, he adds, 'it is evident, in this case, that the impulse *arises not from reason, but is only directed by it. . . . It can never in the least concern us to know, that such objects are causes, and such others effects, if both causes and effects be indifferent to us.'[1]

We have already in some degree considered judgements of this kind in the last chapter. But there is one point which we must re-emphasize here. We have said that, when an end is desired, a judgement about the means whereby it can be achieved influences conduct, because, by directing an already existing desire to the means of its fulfilment, it evokes a desire for the means as well. Our desire for the end is, so to speak, extended to include the means. But Hume is mistaken in supposing that the mere making of a means-ends judgement is, in these conditions, sufficient to evoke this desire. That he sometimes held such a view is evident from the following passage:

'The moment we perceive the falsehood of any supposition', Hume writes, 'or the insufficiency of any means, our passions yield to our reason without any opposition. I may desire any fruit as of excellent relish; but whenever you convince me of my mistake, my longing ceases. I may will the performance of certain actions as means of obtaining any desired good; but as my willing of these actions is only secondary, and founded on the supposition that they are causes of the proposed effect; *as soon as I discover* the falsehood of that supposition they must become indifferent to me.'[2]

We saw in the last chapter that the making of a means-ends judgement, even where the end is desired, is not sufficient to raise a desire for the means. In order that this desire should arise, there must not merely be a desire for the end and awareness of the means, but these two awarenesses must also be

[1] *Treatise*, ii, p. 126 (my italics).          [2] Ibid., p. 128 (my italics).

synthesized in consciousness. The essential need for this act of co-contemplation is overlooked by Hume. He is wrong in thinking that, as soon as we discover that $y$ is a means to $x$, we will come to desire $y$, or that as soon as we discover that $y$ is no means to $x$ our longing for $y$ will cease. In fact, the one or the other will only occur if, in addition to our realizing the relation between means and end, we also think jointly of our desire for the end and of the means as being conducive or not conducive to its attainment.

Turning now from judgements about means to ends to those about the nature of objects, we find that Hume describes these judgements not as 'directing' existing passions but as 'prompting' new ones.[1] It is interesting to note that he did not regard the theoretical *a priori* judgements which we considered in the last chapter in this way, though it is evident that these judgements also are about the nature of objects. When the merchant who owes £100 plus £50 judges that he owes £150, he desires to pay this sum because he already desired to pay the sum total of his debts. Here his judgement, although not about a means to an end, but about the true nature of his debt, is yet said to 'direct' an already existing passion. It is plain that empirical judgements about the nature of objects also can affect action in this way. If I already desire to eat a sweet apple, then when I judge that 'This apple is sweet', my judgement, though about the true nature of an object, will not prompt a new desire, but will direct an old one. When Hume comes to the judgements about the nature of objects which can 'prompt' new passions, he fails to mention that judgements about the nature of objects can, on his own showing, also 'direct' existing ones, but this omission is not a serious one. We have only to note that both empirical and *a priori* judgements about the nature of objects, as well as judgements about means to ends, may direct passions. What is of real interest is Hume's assertion that the former can also have practical influence in another way. The judgement that 'This apple is ripe' can affect my conduct independently of any prior desire to eat an apple of this kind.

[1] Ibid., p. 171.

Now the fact that Hume allows that judgements can have this sort of influence is, prima facie, very surprising. He constantly argues that reason alone cannot cause action, that all action is caused by desire, and further, that reason alone cannot cause desire. And, in the arguments we have considered so far, we have seen that the practical power which he allows to judgements depends always on the relation of these judgements to a pre-existing desire. Now we might well expect that in accordance with his view that judgement alone cannot give rise to desire he would argue that the only judgements which influence action are directive ones. For, if a judgement cannot merely direct an existing passion but can also prompt a new one, then we may well be tempted to think that desire can be determined by 'reason alone' as its sufficient cause. We have therefore to ask precisely what Hume meant when he said that judgements about the nature of objects can *prompt* passions. But, in order to do this, it will be necessary to inquire further into his general views about the origins of action.

We have already observed that according to Hume all actions are caused by desires or motives. It is true that he nowhere specifically defines action as movement which is caused in this way, but he does argue that all actions have particular causes. He concludes the sections 'Of Liberty and Necessity' by saying that 'having proved that all actions of the will have particular causes, I proceed to explain what these causes are, and how they operate'.[1] And in the following section which is called 'Of the Influencing Motives of the Will' he maintains that all motives are desires. Thus the problem of what causes action is for Hume the problem of what causes desire. Now Hume classes desire along with all other passions as what he calls 'an impression of reflection'.[2] Passions are 'simple impressions' to

---

[1] *Treatise*, ii, p. 125.

[2] See ibid., i, p. 16: 'Impressions may be divided into two kinds, those of *sensation*, and those of *reflection*. The first kind arises in the soul originally, from unknown causes. The second is derived, in a great measure, from our ideas, and that in the following order. An impression first strikes upon the senses, and makes us perceive heat or cold, thirst or hunger, pleasure or pain, of some kind or other. Of this impression there is a copy taken by the mind, which remains after the impression ceases; and this we call an idea. This idea

which no multitude of words can give definition.[1] They can be caused by either ideas or impressions, but normally, he thinks, they are caused by ideas. In fact it is clear that those passions which are desires are always caused by ideas; for, though Hume does not explicitly make this point, they are caused by the thoughts of their objects; and, since we cannot desire what already exists, our 'perception' of these objects must be ideas and not impressions. Our desire to do any particular act, then, is caused by the idea of this act.[2] But it does not follow that all ideas of acts give rise to a desire to do them. Whether any given idea causes desire or not depends on the instinctive dispositions of the agent. Hume considers that, on the whole, our instincts incline us to do those acts which we believe will be accompanied by sensations of pleasure. Desires, therefore, are normally caused by the thought of acts as pleasurable, but not exclusively so.

'It is easy to observe', he writes, 'that the passions, both direct and indirect, are founded on pain and pleasure, and that, in order to produce an affection of any kind, it is only requisite to present some good or evil.... The impressions which arise from good and evil most naturally ... are the *direct* passions of desire and aversion, grief and joy, hope and fear. . . .'[3]

But to this he adds that,

'Besides good and evil, or, in other words, pain and pleasure, the direct passions frequently arise from a natural impulse or instinct, which is perfectly unaccountable. Of this kind is the desire of punish-

of pleasure or pain, when it returns upon the soul, produces the new impressions of desire and aversion, hope and fear, which may properly be called impressions of reflection, because derived from it.'

[1] Ibid., ii, p. 5.

[2] Hume points out that in the case of pride and humility the idea which excites the passion is not the idea of its object. 'We must ... make a distinction betwixt the cause and object of these passions; betwixt that idea which excites them, and that to which they direct their view when excited.' Ibid., p. 6. He does not consider this question at all when he comes to the direct passions; desires and aversions. But it is obvious that in this case the reverse is true. A desire is always caused by the thought of that which is desired. The idea which excites this passion is precisely the idea of that 'to which they direct their view when excited'. Their cause is the idea of their object.

[3] Ibid., p. 147.

ment to our enemies, and of happiness to our friends; hunger, lust, and a few other bodily appetites.'[1]

We can conclude, then, that according to Hume, actions are caused by desire, and desires are caused by such ideas as, on account of our original instincts, have the power of causing them.[2]

We are now in a position to answer our question: What did Hume mean by saying that judgements about the nature of objects can prompt passions, and how was he able to hold this view side by side with his theory that reason alone cannot cause either passions or actions? It is plain that if desires are caused by ideas, then these desires can be indirectly caused by any judgements which determine the nature of those ideas which are before the mind at any given time. If I am the kind of

---

[1] *Treatise*, ii, p. 148. Hume continues: 'The mind by an *original* instinct tends to unite itself with the good and avoid the evil.'

[2] A similar conception of action was held by Hobbes. But Hobbes, unlike Hume, explicitly defines action, or what he calls 'animal motion'. Moreover, Hobbes explicitly holds a view which it seems likely that Hume held also, though he nowhere discusses it, namely, that desires are not so much the causes of actions as part of them. Actions, according to Hobbes, are caused by ideas and the beginnings of these actions are desires. Hobbes expresses his view of action so clearly that it is worth quoting. See *Leviathan, Of Man*, ch. 6, 'Of the Interior Beginnings of Voluntary Motions: commonly called the Passions.' Hobbes writes as follows: 'There be, in animals, two sorts of *motions* peculiar to them: one called *vitall*; begun in generation, and continued without interruption through their whole life; such as are the *course* of the *bloud*, the *pulse*, the *breathing*, the *concoction, nutrition, excretion*, etc.: to which motions there needs no help of the imagination: The other is *animall motion*, otherwise called *voluntary motion*; as to *go*, to *speak*, to *move* any of our limbs in such manner as is first fancied in our minds. That sense is motion in the organs and interior parts of mans body, caused by the action of things we see, heare, *etc.*: And that fancy is but the reliques of the same motion, remaining after Sense, has been already seen in the first and second Chapters. [Compare this with Hume's theory of impressions of reflection. Hobbes's sense, which corresponds to Hume's impressions of sensation, though he accounts for it very differently, leaves behind it fancies, which correspond to Hume's ideas, and these in their turn are the cause of passions and desires.] And because *going*, *speaking*, and the like voluntary motions, depend alwayes on the precedent thought, of *whither, which way* and *what*; it is evident that the imagination is the first internal beginning of all voluntary motion. . . . These small beginnings of motion within the body of man, before they appear in walking, speaking, striking, and other visible actions, are commonly called *endeavour*.

'This endeavour, when it is toward something which causes it, is called *appetite* or *desire*, . . . When the endeavour is fromward something, it is generally called Aversion.'

person who likes eating ripe apples, that is to say, if I have a disposition to desire to eat ripe apples, then the judgement 'This is a ripe apple' will cause desire. It will do so by bringing the idea of a ripe apple before my mind, and its effect will be independent of any pre-existent desire to eat such an apple. Thus any judgement which makes the agent aware of the nature of an object can cause him to desire this object, if he is the kind of person who is affected with desire by the thought of such objects. But these judgements, equally with those that direct passions, are not by themselves the causes of desire. The desire's immediate cause is the idea and not the judgement which brings this idea before the mind. Moreover, whether any given idea, once it is before the mind, will cause desire or not, is independent of our reason and judgement. It depends solely on our instincts. No judgement can enable an idea to have effect, if the agent is by nature such that he is intrinsically indifferent to the thought of it. Thus Hume's two views that judgements alone cannot cause passions, and that judgements can 'prompt' passions, are not, after all, incompatible.

Now the assertion that judgements can 'prompt' passions is both interesting and suggestive. Judgements, Hume maintains, can cause new passions, and can eliminate existing ones, by varying the information which an agent possesses, at any given time, and this information need not relate to desires which he already has. But interesting though this view is, we may well wish that Hume had expounded it more fully, for it raises certain questions which he leaves unanswered, and in several respects it does not seem to be precise.

First we must note a point which may appear puzzling. Hume, as we have seen, maintains that ideas which give rise to passions are normally ideas of pleasurable actions, and that the judgements which prompt passions are normally judgements about 'the prospect of pleasure or pain' which 'we have from any object'. But we may well wonder why he regarded these judgements as different from judgements about means to ends. The judgement that '$x$ will give pleasure' certainly looks as though it were of the form '$x$ is a means to $y$', rather than of the form '$x$ is of the kind $y$'.[1] It is, I think, commonly assumed that judgements about the pleasure-giving qualities of acts are judgements about means to ends. But if this were the case, all such judgements would direct passions and none would prompt them. For in order to be affected by the judgement that '$x$ is a means to pleasure' it would be necessary for pleasure to be already desired. But in fact, I think, we should be mistaken in assuming that judgements about acts giving pleasure are normally judgements about means to ends. Hume certainly did not take this view. He evidently did not regard pleasure as an end to which certain pleasure-giving acts are means. On the contrary he thought that the pleasantness of acts was *part of them* and not something separate to which they must be regarded as conducive. In this he seems to be right. It is true that if we think of an act as an external event, then as such it is certainly separable from the feelings of pleasure which it occasions in the agent who performs it. It is for this reason that we are able to speak of it as *giving* pleasure, or as *accompanied by* pleasant sensations. But if we regard the act from the point of view of the agent, that is, as it is for him, then it and the feelings to which it gives rise are not two separate entities but one entity which is characterized in a special way. When I think of *my* riding a horse I do not think of the feeling which I shall have when riding it as something which is caused by riding a horse, but as part of it; these feelings pertain to the nature of my act, they are numbered not among its relational but among its intrinsic properties. It is for this reason that statements about the pleasantness of actions can be made in two ways. We can say, on the one hand, that an act gives or is conducive to pleasure, and on the other that it is itself pleasant or pleasurable. In the first case, we are thinking of the act as an event in the external world—as it would be regarded by others; in the second, we are thinking of it as a state of ourselves: in the first case there are two events which we relate, in the second there is one event which we qualify; there are

---

[1] I am assuming here that means-ends judgements are properly about a kind of material implication. See above, Chapter III, pp. 92 ff.

two events in the external world, but there is only one state of myself. It is acts categorized in the second manner which are the objects of desire. To be affected by the judgement 'Riding a horse is pleasant' is to be affected by a judgement which is different in form from the judgement 'Riding a horse gives me a pain in the back', or 'If I ride a horse I shall be shopping in Porlock this afternoon'. That this is so is confirmed by the fact that it is sensible to say 'Riding a horse *is* pleasant', whereas the statements 'Riding a horse *is* painful in the back' or 'Riding a horse *is* shopping in Porlock' are nonsensical. It follows that, since feeling pleasure is not a separate thing to which doing an act gives rise, in order to be affected by the judgement that a certain act is pleasurable it is not always necessary to synthesize this judgement with a pre-existing desire for pleasure. This would only be the case if pleasure judgements were about a means to an end or some other kind of material implication.[1] This is not to say that judgements about the pleasurableness of acts do not sometimes give rise to desire by directing an already existing passion, but that this is not the only nor, indeed, the more normal way for them to have effect.

The second point which we have to notice is that the judgements to which Hume refers as 'prompting' passions are judgements about *objects*. That is to say he is referring here to judgements like 'This *apple* is ripe', or 'The *train* from Reading to Basingstoke is unheated during war time', or '*Tang horses* are objects of great beauty.' But strictly speaking, judgements about objects do not themselves prompt passions, for they do not bring before our minds any ideas which in themselves can cause desire. Desires are caused by ideas not of objects but of *actions*. The idea of an apple, or a train, or a Tang horse, cannot itself give rise to a desire however specific and articulate it may be. The ideas which cause desires are the ideas not of apples but of eating them, or making jam of them, not of trains but of travelling by train, not of Tang horses but

---

[1] Judgements about process and constituent can also only direct passions, but plainly pleasure judgements are not of this kind. '*x* is pleasant' could not possibly mean '*x* is a constituent of a peculiar process'.

of looking at Tang horses, of coming to possess them, or of keeping them in our possession. It is our judgements about what these actions would be like, or the possibility of doing them, which bring before our minds those ideas which give rise to desire. On the other hand, it is certainly true that judgements about the nature of objects may indirectly cause desire, for they may lead us to form ideas of acts connected with these objects, either associatively or as the result of inquiry. The remark 'There are Tang horses in the Ashmolean' may by association give rise to the idea of *looking at* Tang horses or of *stealing* them. The judgement 'There are windfalls in the orchard' may lead me to ask myself: *What can be done* with windfalls? And as the result of making this inquiry I may form the idea of *making* apple chutney. But in either case the judgement about the object will only give rise to an idea which can cause desire if some further mental process takes place.

Yet we have to qualify Hume's position still farther. For it is evident that the idea which causes my desire must not only be about *an* action but about *my* action. It is not the judgements 'Tang horses can be seen in the Ashmolean' or 'Windfalls can be made into apple chutney' which are capable of prompting passion, but the judgements 'If I were to go to the Ashmolean I should see a Tang horse' or 'I could make these windfalls into apple chutney.' The descriptions in the *Oxford Mail* of people looking at Tang horses and the instructions for making apple chutney in Mrs. Beeton are in themselves ineffectual, though they may have an indirect effect, for they too may be connected by association with the idea of my looking at Tang horses or my making apple chutney.

With these reservations we can agree with Hume's view that judgements about the nature of objects prompt desire. And yet even then we must admit that his account of their influence, although suggestive, is far from adequate. We have already seen that in the case of judgements about means to ends he thought that it was sufficient merely to make these judgements, and ignored altogether the necessity of *synthesizing* them with already existing desires. And here, too, he thinks that action will be prompted, if at all, as soon as the judgement is made. Yet evidently this is not the case. It is true indeed that here there is no need for *synthesis*, for these judgements are effective independently of *pre-existing* desires. Yet it is a matter of common experience that they do not always have the influence of which they are intrinsically capable. Very often they have no influence, not because the nature of the agent is such that he is *incapable* of being affected by them, but because certain other conditions remain unfulfilled. A full description of these conditions would be too long and too complex for the present book. But we must try to enumerate them as briefly as possible.

There is one point which we have first to call attention to. It is that when Hume speaks of the practical influence of theoretical judgements he always considers them as concerned with the *truth* or *falsehood* of the propositions which we believe to be true about the objects of our desire. A passion is unreasonable if it is founded on a false supposition about its object, it is reasonable if founded on a true one. Hume assumes, at least in this part of the *Treatise*, that if we are affected by the conception of an object or action, then a judgement can only change the way in which we are affected by showing that our conception is mistaken. I am prevented from eating a fruit which I had previously supposed to be 'of excellent relish' by the judgement that the fruit has not this property. This judgement shows that my previous supposition was wrong. Hume overlooks altogether the possibility that our conceptions of acts may not only be *mistaken* but also *inadequate*. I may have an idea of an act as possessed of one quality, and the proposition that it has this quality may be true, and yet a further judgement or judgements about this act may still change the way in which I am affected by the idea of it. For such judgements, by showing that the act has also other qualities, may modify and yet not falsify my previous conception. Thus I can suppose that an apple is ripe, and I may be quite right in thinking so, and yet my feelings towards this apple may be changed by the further judgement that it is also full of wasps. In this case it would be wrong to say that my previous idea was mistaken, or that it rested on a belief in a false proposition. In so far as it went it was a 'true' idea, but it did not go far enough. The further judgements which I may make about an object do not turn a 'false' idea into a 'true' one, they make more adequate an idea which was previously 'true' but inadequate. Our idea is, then, founded not on our knowledge of a true proposition instead of a false one, but on a greater number of true ones. With this in mind we may now turn to examine those conditions which must be fulfilled if a judgement about the nature of an action is to prompt a desire to do it.

Now it is evident that some judgements go farther than others in elucidating the natures of objects, or of actions which are connected with these objects, and that in cases where the elucidatory function of a judgement is very limited the idea which we form as the result of making it may be very inadequate. Here the idea may fail to cause that desire which it would cause if it were more adequate, or it may cause aversion where it would otherwise cause desire, or desire where it would otherwise cause aversion. In Hume's example the judgement goes a long way in elucidating its object: the judgement that I can now eat a fruit of excellent relish brings before my mind a fairly adequate idea, although even here I might be affected differently if I made further judgements. But there are judgements which contribute so little to the forming of an adequate idea that they may be unable to move us at all. This would be the case if I were to judge for instance that it was now possible for me to go on an expedition to Mount Everest. Unless it so happened that I had previously made many judgements about what going on this kind of expedition would be like, this judgement would not give rise to either desire or aversion until a great many other judgements had been made. The judgement by itself would fail to affect me even though I were the sort of person who would want to go on an expedition to Everest if I knew what such an expedition would be like. For the power of such judgements to cause desire consists in the fact that they bring before consciousness the ideas of possible actions in a certain degree of clarity, but if this degree of clarity is small, then they will have no effect until further similar judgements have been made. Moreover my desires will vary with the kind of further judgements that are made, and even after I have made a great many, it will still be possible for another judgement to reverse the effect of the previous ones. Thus having judged that it is possible for me to go on an expedition to Everest, I may go on to judge that such an expedition will consist in a pleasant sea journey, a ride on yaks across Sikkim, much climbing, and being in pleasant company, and in view of these judgements I may desire to go. And yet the single judgement that in approaching Everest men are normally bitten by leeches may reverse the effect of all previous ones and I may develop an intense aversion to taking part in any such expedition.

One condition, then, which must be fulfilled before some theoretical judgements can prompt passion is that these judgements should be followed by others of the same kind. It is impossible to enter on a full discussion of this condition here. Such an analysis would involve us in a consideration of choice and of other mental processes which Hume never considered. We can only call attention to the fact that the ways in which a series of judgements about some complex action prompt us to desire this action are very intricate. About an act like going on an expedition to Everest we can make a vast number of judgements: some will exert an attracting influence, some a repelling one, and others will have no effect at all until further judgements about the nature of *their* objects have been made. The more true judgements we make, the more adequate our idea of the act will become, the less susceptible to change will be the desire which it raises, and the less likely will the agent be to regret the action when it is done. The more adequate our idea of an act the less capricious our desire to do it. We can say that when we are determined by an inadequate idea we are determined *subjectively*, for the effects of this idea depend upon the fact that the idea is formed as the result of making inadequate judgements; it is determined, that is to say, by purely subjective forces which cause us to overlook the real nature of the act. When we are determined by an adequate idea, on the other hand, we are determined *objectively*, for here our idea conforms to the real nature of the object.

The other conditions which enable judgements about the nature of acts to take effect need not detain us long. They are concerned with the time during which the idea which results from the judgement remains before the mind, and the degree of attention which it then receives, that is to say the extent to which it is before the mind to the exclusion of other ideas. It is plain that a judgement will have no effect if the idea which it presents to consciousness does no more than pass fleetingly through the mind even though it is the kind of idea which would affect the agent if he had attended to it for long enough. This case may be compared to that where I pass my finger through a flame. The flame is the kind of thing which would burn my finger if it were to remain there for a sufficient period, but it has no perceptible effect if I merely pass my finger through. Again, an idea may be before the mind for a considerable period and yet may not have the effect of which it is intrinsically capable, for we may at the same time entertain other and contrary ideas whose effect neutralizes that of the first. This case may be compared with that where I hold my finger in a flame for a considerable time, but at the same time pour water on it.

Hence in addition to the favourableness of our instincts, three conditions must be fulfilled if any idea is to cause a desire: the idea must be sufficiently articulated, it must be before the mind for a sufficient time, and it must receive sufficient attention. Any judgement about the nature of an object may fail to have effect because the idea to which it gives rise does not meet with these conditions.

Having considered the influence of empirical judgements up to this point we are in a position to make a preliminary survey of Hume's whole doctrine of reason as the cause of action. Reason or judgement can, according to Hume, only affect action by regulating the ideas which are before the mind: that is by determinining what passions and volitions are operative in an agent at any given time by presenting to him the ideas which are capable of giving rise to them. It is not possible for reason to cause acts directly, for all acts are directly caused by desire. Nor is it possible for reason to cause desires directly, for desires are caused by ideas. Nor can it cause ideas which are fully before the mind to give rise to desires, for the power of an idea to cause desire is dependent solely upon our instincts, and our instincts are wholly beyond our control. But reason and judgement can, up to a point, determine what ideas are before our minds. By reflection and judgement we can become aware both of the relation of certain acts to others which are already desired and of the possibility of doing acts which are of a certain kind. This doctrine is central to the whole of Hume's practical philosophy; so central that it merits being called by a special name. We might, I think, call it the *doctrine of reason as the 'mediate' or 'oblique' cause of action*. For Hume writes that 'reason and judgement may, indeed, be the mediate cause of an action by prompting or directing a passion',[1] and again that an action may 'obliquely' be caused by a judgement.[2]

It is a consequence of this view that Hume's assertion that reason alone cannot cause action—important though it is in limiting the sphere within which reason can be practical—can only be taken as limiting, and not as eliminating it.

With the foregoing arguments in mind we may now look briefly at those passages where Hume uses his most blatantly anti-rationalist language. Here he denies emphatically not merely that reason alone can cause a passion, but also that it can ever oppose an existing one. The supposed 'combat between passion and reason' and the 'pre-eminence of reason above passion' on which the 'greatest part of moral philosophy, ancient and modern seems to be founded'[3] is, he declares, entirely fictitious. For if judgement alone cannot cause a passion, then neither can it prevent one. A desire can only be counteracted by another and contrary desire, and since reason alone cannot give rise to the first desire, neither can it give rise

---

[1] *Treatise*, ii, p. 171.     [2] Ibid., p. 168.     [3] Ibid., p. 125.

to the desire which opposes it. Hence reason alone cannot oppose any passion. Hume states his position with great clarity:

'Since reason alone can never produce any action, or give rise to volition, I infer, that the same faculty is as incapable of preventing volition, or of disputing the preference with any passion or emotion. This consequence is necessary. It is impossible reason could have the latter effect of preventing volition, but by giving an impulse in a contrary direction to our passions; and that impulse, had it operated alone, would have been ample to produce volition. Nothing can oppose or retard the impulse of passion, but a contrary impulse; and if this contrary impulse ever arises from reason, that latter faculty must have an original influence on the will, and must be able to cause, as well as hinder, any act of volition.'[1]

It is evident, however, that Hume is not here denying that the passion which opposes another, equally with the original passion, can have reason or judgement as its mediate cause.[2] Indeed we may say that up to this point Hume's anti-rationalism is of a very moderate kind. He seeks to destroy the assumption that judgement by itself can cause action, but

[1] *Treatise*, ii, p. 126.

[2] It is interesting to recall in this connexion two passages which occur in Spinoza and one in Bacon's *Advancement of Learning*. The passages from Spinoza we shall have occasion to quote again in the next chapter, yet they compare so interestingly in this connexion that we must also call attention to them here.

Proposition VII in Part IV of the *Ethics* reads as follows: 'Affectus coerceri nec tolli potest, nisi per affectum contrarium et fortiorem affectu coercendo'; and Proposition XIV: 'Vera boni et mali cognitio, quatenus vera, nullum affectum coercere potest, sed tantum quatenus ut affectus consideratur.' These passages are unequivocal and are central to Spinoza's practical philosophy. The remarks on this subject in Bacon are less important, moreover Bacon does not say that passions can only be controlled by contrary passions, but that this is a convenient way of controlling them. None the less his remark is interesting: 'It is', he says, 'of speciall use in morale and civile matters', to know how '*to set affection against affection; and by the helpe of one to master and reclaime another.* After the manner of hunters and fowlers, who hunt beast with beast; and fly bird with bird; which percase of themselves without the assistance of bruit creatures, a man could not so easily recover. Nay farther, upon this foundation is errected that excellent and universall use in matters civile of *praemium* and *poena*, which are the *pillars of civile states*; seeing those *predominant affections* of *feare* and *hope* doe bridle and suppress all other exorbitant *affections*. Again, as in government of states, it is sometimes necessary to confront and bridle one faction with another; so it is in the inward *government of the minde.*' *Advancement of Learning*, Book VIII, ch. iii. Compare this with Hume's arguments about justice. See below, pp. 123 ff.

his arguments do not show that judgement is of no practical importance. They do no more than limit the field of its operation to that within which it can be properly explained, understood, and defended by sound philosophical argument.

But it is precisely at this point that Hume introduces his famous argument that 'reason is, and ought only to be, the slave of the passions'. The passage quoted above concludes with the remark that reason can never 'keep the mind in suspense a moment. . . . We speak not strictly and philosophically, when we talk of the combat of passion and of reason. Reason is, and ought only to be, the slave of the passions, and can never pretend to any other office than to serve and obey them.'[1] In part, this view implies no more than that which we have already considered. We have seen that by saying that there is no combat between reason and passion, but only between one passion and another, Hume is asserting that all combat is ultimately between passions, though the passions which contend with one another may be mediately caused by judgement. This view follows from his definitions of action and desire, and with it we cannot but agree. Moreover, in saying that reason is the servant of the passions he is clearly referring to his view that reason can do no more than supply the mind with data—knowledge of the nature of possible acts and knowledge of causes and effects—which our instinctive dispositions may or may not make use of, but which will have no effect unless they do so. In so far as this is his meaning he is not denying that reason can influence our actions, he is only reiterating his old view that what influence reason has is ultimately dependent on our existing passions, which are directed, or our potential passions, which are aroused. As Professor Laird remarks, Hume 'regarded reason as an astute family solicitor rather than as an ordinary sort of slave'.[2] Yet, in fact, Hume's remarks that reason is not merely the *servant* but also the *slave* of the passions, that it not merely *serves* but also *obeys* them, are of a more sinister kind. His reference here seems to be, not to the limits which

[1] *Treatise*, ii, p. 127.
[2] John Laird, Hume's *Philosophy of Human Nature*, p. 204.

are imposed on the influence of judgement by the fact that this influence is always dependent upon our natural dispositions, but to the fact that, since judging is itself acting, reasoning and judging must themselves be caused by a passion. The efficacy of judgement will depend, not merely on the impulses which judgements direct or the instincts which interest us in the ideas to which judgements give rise, but also, and indeed ultimately, upon the impulses which prompt us to make these judgements in the first place. The implications of Hume's argument here are of rather a complex nature and will need considering at some length. We shall leave them till the next chapter.

We have now said all that it is necessary to say about Hume's account of the practical influence of empirical *theoretical* judgements. We must now turn to the influence of empirical *practical* judgements. We noted in the last chapter that if Hume's critique of the rationalists was to be complete, he could not afford to ignore the problem of practical judgements. For the rationalists maintained at least implicitly that human conduct was regulated by such judgements, and further, that they could be made *a priori*—though it is true that their reference to them was often confused and misleading.[1] Hume, as we have seen, while admitting that theoretical *a priori* judgements can influence action, denied emphatically that any practical judgements can be *a priori*. But his arguments there, although conclusive within their own sphere of reference, were yet not sufficient to refute the rationalists' position as a whole. For it may still pertinently be asked whether their mistake lay in supposing that it is possible to make practical judgements at all, or merely in supposing that such judgements can be *a priori*. Hume, as we have seen, has shown that practical judgements cannot be *a priori*, but there remains the question of whether they can be empirical. Any critique of the rationalist position would be incomplete so long as this question remained unanswered.

Now we have to admit from the start that Hume did not

---

[1] See above, Chapters I and II.

explicitly ask himself this question. He evidently thought that he had answered the Clarkians sufficiently when he had pointed out that, despite the indirect influence of both *a priori* and empirical judgements, it was wholly impossible to maintain that *a priori* judgements have a direct influence. There are no practical *a priori* judgements. Moreover, if we do not look beyond the later sections of the second book and the earlier sections of the third, we may argue with some plausibility that, if Hume had asked himself this question, he would have answered it in the negative. For in these sections he not only limits his consideration of judgements which have practical influence to those whose influence is incidental to them, but he goes so far as to assert that these are the only judgements which can influence action at all. We have seen in Chapter II that he undertook his inquiry into the relation between reason and conduct because he thought that if reason cannot influence conduct then neither can it be the basis of morality. We have now seen that, within the context of this inquiry, he allows that there are judgements which have an incidental effect on conduct. But he hastens to conclude that this is not the kind of influence which a judgement would have to have if it were a moral one. Moral judgements, if there are any, are certainly not about facts which are external to the agent, and if the only judgements which can influence action are about these facts, moral conduct must be independent of judgements and of reason. Our judgements about means to ends and about the nature of objects or actions may be mistaken, but to act on such erroneous judgements is not to behave immorally:

'. . . it is easy to observe', Hume writes, 'that these errors are so far from being the source of all immorality, that they are commonly very innocent, and draw no manner of guilt upon the person who is so unfortunate as to fall into them. They extend not beyond a mistake of *fact*, which moralists have not generally supposed criminal, as being perfectly involuntary. I am more to be lamented than blamed, if I am mistaken with regard to the influence of objects in producing pain or pleasure, or if I know not the proper means of satisfying my desires.'[1]

[1] *Treatise*, ii, p. 169. See also p. 171: 'Reason and judgement may, indeed, be the mediate cause of an action, by prompting or by directing a passion; but

Hume's argument here is certainly valid. Judgements of external fact, such as he here describes, cannot be moral judgements, for they are not practical, and moral judgements, in so far as they are judgements about obligations, must be practical even though not all practical judgements need be moral. It is evident that we do not call people's actions immoral when they rest on mistakes about such facts. What we call immoral in their conduct is, if anything, not that they make an erroneous judgement of external fact, but that they have failed to act in accordance with such judgements, and also that they have failed to make them. I am certainly 'more to be lamented than blamed' if I get on a train which in fact goes to Birmingham when I wanted to go to London and judged that this train would take me there. But if I want to go to London and judge that this train will take me there, I may be blamed for not 'making up my mind' to take it, that is, for not making the judgement that, 'Since I want to go to London, and this train will take me there, I must on reflection, be ready to take this train'.

In this part of the *Treatise* Hume overlooks this possibility altogether, as is made amply evident by the fact that he continues the above argument in the following way:

'A fruit, for instance, that is really disagreeable, appears to me at a distance, and, through mistake, I fancy it to be pleasant and delicious. Here is one error. I choose certain means of reaching this fruit, which are not proper for my end. Here is a second error; nor is there any third one, which can ever possibly enter into our reasonings concerning actions. I ask, therefore, if a man in this situation, and guilty of these two errors, is to be regarded as vicious and criminal, however unavoidable they might have been? Or if it is possible to imagine that such errors are the sources of all immorality?'[1]

Here Hume, by implication, denies that there can be practical judgements. There is, he says, 'no third error which can ever enter into our reasonings concerning actions'.

But although from these earlier passages we should be tempted to conclude that had Hume asked himself whether

it is not pretended that a judgement of this kind, either in its truth or falsehood, is attended with virtue or vice.'

[1] *Treatise*, ii, p. 169.

there can be empirical practical judgements he would have answered that such judgements are altogether impossible, yet this is not the conclusion which is suggested by the *Treatise* as a whole. For here as elsewhere Hume begins his argument by establishing relatively narrow general principles which he is forced to expand and elaborate when he comes to apply them to particular instances, but he does not subsequently amend these principles as such. In this case we find that, in considering the problem of how we come to desire certain particular actions, he is forced to develop his whole theory of the practical influence of empirical judgements and to develop it in such a way that in doing so he admits the possibility of practical judgements. But he never reverts to his general inquiry and adds that there is a third error which can enter into our reasoning concerning actions.

We must now consider this application of Hume's general theory, so that we may discover the degree to which he in fact admits that there are some empirical judgements which cannot be made without affecting our passions, and the way in which this admission is forced upon him. Here it will once more be convenient to divide our argument into two parts. Hume, as we have seen, thought that the theoretical judgements which influence action are of two kinds: those which direct passions and those which prompt them. In considering his views about practical judgements we must make a similar division. We must consider first the implications which his various arguments have for the possibility of practical *directive* judgements, and secondly the implications they have for the possibility of what we shall call practical *promptive* or *incentive* ones. We have to ask whether, in view of Hume's other arguments, he would have given an affirmative answer *first* to the question: Can we make judgements about what it would be necessary for us to do on reflection in view of our existing desires and our present information? And *secondly* to the question: Can we make judgements about what it would be necessary for us to do on reflection in view of the intrinsic nature of the actions that are open to us and our own instinctive dispositions?

In seeking an answer to the first of these questions we must turn to the sections on the 'artificial virtues'. These sections play a central part in Hume's exposition of his moral philosophy. He does in fact devote more space to them than to the 'natural' ones, and he is evidently more interested in them. It is here that we find his analysis of the obligations to keep promises, to respect property, and to obey the laws of the state, as well as those to chastity and modesty, and his account of international law. These sections are of the greatest importance for our problem. The view of the relation between reason and conduct which Hume takes here is, at least prima facie, very different from that which he takes in the passages we have so far considered. First, he lays an entirely different emphasis on the practical importance of theoretical judgements. And secondly, the influence which he allows to reason here is in part influence of a new kind. It is evident that in the earlier sections he was concerned to minimize the importance of reason, for there his arguments had a negative purpose. Reason, he had to admit, has certain powers, but his intention was to show that these powers are far more confined than certain of his predecessors had supposed. Here, on the other hand, his purpose is quite different: it is to show how we come to be moved to certain acts to which we are not moved by any 'natural' disposition, and in this argument the practical powers of reason have a positive significance. There are here, he argues, two principles which govern our conduct, the affections and the understanding:

'Human nature', he writes, 'being composed of two principle parts, which are requisite in all its actions, the affections and understanding, it is certain that the blind motions of the former, without the direction of the latter, incapacitate men for society; . . .'[1]

It may be that the functions of the understanding to which Hume here refers are merely those which he considered earlier. But there are passages in these sections which show that these were not the only functions of the understanding that he had in mind. For he argues that with the help of the understand-

[1] *Treatise*, ii, p. 198.

ing we formulate *laws* or *rules of conduct*. We become aware
that certain actions are our 'natural obligations': that it is
necessary for us to do some acts and to refrain from doing
others. Our awareness of this necessity vitally affects our conduct, and it is on this awareness that the whole structure of
social life depends. It is evident that the judgements whereby
we formulate such *rules* and become aware of our *obligations*
are not the mere judgements of fact which Hume considered
earlier: they are, as we shall see, not theoretical, but practical
empirical judgements.

Hume's problem in the sections on the artificial virtues is
briefly as follows: We have, according to him, motives to respect property, to keep our promises, and to obey the laws of
the state: we in fact normally do these things, and yet it is
evident that our motives in doing them are not 'natural'. We
have no natural instincts which could prompt us to behave in
these ways. Our strongest instinct is self love, 'But it is certain
that self-love, when it acts at its liberty, instead of engaging us
to honest actions, is the source of all injustice and violence; ...'[1]
Moreover, though we have a natural affection for those who
are near to us, our love of them could not prompt us to act
justly, for justice is often contrary to the interest of individuals.
Nor, Hume argues, are we prompted to these acts by any
general affection for mankind as such, for, 'In general it
may be affirmed, that there is no such passion in human
minds as the love of mankind, merely as such, ...'[2] Yet
it is evident that we are moved to respect property, to keep
promises and to obey laws, and indeed not merely that we
are moved to acts of this kind, but that we think we are *obliged*
to do them. What then are the motives which govern this
behaviour?

Hume's answer to this question is that our motives here are
the products not of natural passions but of *reason*. At the same
time he makes it plain that in so saying he is not reverting to the
position of the *a priori* school. He does not argue that reason
where it gives rise to passions does so by itself and indepen-

[1] Ibid., p. 187.                          [2] Ibid.

dently of our natural dispositions. He is in fact careful to guard himself against the charge of such a recantation.

'. . . the sense of justice', he points out, 'is not founded on reason, or on the discovery of certain connections and relations of ideas, which are eternal, immutable, and universally obligatory.'[1]

The judgements which give rise to our desires are the judgements about means to ends, which he has described in the earlier sections: they are the judgements which *direct* our existing passions: judgements about the way to achieve the ends which we naturally desire, but which we could not achieve without making these judgements about the way to achieve them. According to Hume, the many instinctive desires of man for his pleasures and happiness, that is his 'interested affections', are such that they could not be fulfilled if he did not live in society. Yet in order to live in society we have to behave in a way which we would never desire for its own sake, hence our motives in so behaving cannot be attributed to our natural dispositions when these are unaided by reason:

'In vain', Hume writes, 'should we expect to find, in *uncultivated nature*, a remedy to this inconvenience. . . . The remedy, then, is not derived from nature, but from *artifice*; or, more properly speaking, nature provides a remedy, in the judgement and understanding, for what is irregular and incommodious in the affections.'[2]

Throughout this argument Hume persistently points out that the function of judgement and understanding here is purely directive. Our desires for pleasure and happiness are, he thinks, so strong that they could not be counteracted by any other passion, and all that reasoning does is to give a new direction to these passions by pointing out the ways in which they can best be fulfilled. Our desire for property, for instance, is better satisfied when we respect the possessions of others than when we steal them, and our judgement that this is so directs our desire to possess:

'There is', Hume writes, 'no passion, therefore, capable of controlling the interested affection, but the very affection itself,[3] by an alteration

---

[1] *Treatise*, ii, p. 200.    [2] Ibid., p. 193.
[3] This is evidently an empirical generalization. Hume has argued with great

of its direction. Now, this alteration must necessarily take place upon the least reflection; since it is evident that the passion is much better satisfied by its restraint than by its liberty, and that, in preserving society, we make much greater advances in the acquiring possessions, than in the solitary and forlorn condition which must follow upon violence and an universal licence.'[1]

This passage must be taken together with another which reads:

'Nor is such a restraint contrary to these passions; for, if so, it could never be entered into nor maintained; but it is only contrary to their heedless and impetuous movement. Instead of departing from our own interest, or from that of our nearest friends, by abstaining from the possessions of others, we cannot better consult both these interests than by such a convention; because it is by that means we maintain society, which is so necessary to their well-being and subsistence, as well as to our own.'[2]

Thus far we can say that Hume's argument in these sections is merely an application of his previous theory that theoretical judgements about means to ends direct existing passions.[3] But as yet we have not considered the whole of Hume's argument, for he maintains also that in this case such judgements terminate in the formation of rules or laws which are concerned with the necessity of adopting the means which they specify.

'. . . everyone who has any regard to his character, or who intends to live on good terms with mankind, *must fix an inviolable law to himself*, never, by any temptation, to be induced to violate those principles which are essential to a man of probity and honour.'[4]

---

vigour that we cannot say *a priori* what is desired, and it follows that we cannot say *a priori* what desires are the stronger.

[1] Ibid., p. 197.                    [2] Ibid., p. 195.

[3] From the above passages it is abundantly clear that Hume is not here in any way abandoning his general position that all actions are caused by desires and that reason can be no more than the mediate cause of action. He has maintained throughout that reason *can* be the mediate cause of action, and he does no more than reassert this here. The actions with which he is concerned in the chapters on the artificial virtues are all *mediately* caused by reason and *immediately* caused by passion. It would not be necessary to press this point but for the fact that certain philosophers have argued that Hume's account of the artificial virtues is totally incompatible with his account of the origin of action, whereas in fact it is evidently part of this account. How far Hume's doctrine of the influence of reason on conduct has been misunderstood is evident from Hedenius, *Studies in Hume's Ethics*, p. 440.

[4] *Treatise*, ii, p. 205 (my italics).

Moreover, Hume refers to *obligations* to act justly, and he calls these obligations the *Laws of Nature*. In fact, in this part of the *Treatise* he revives the old natural law doctrine, while at the same time making it evident that these laws rest on an empirical basis only. They state a necessity of behaving in a certain way, but their validity rests on empirical premisses. For they are valid only so long as our desires and the means to their fulfilment remain the same: 'an alteration . . . in the temper and circumstances of mankind, would entirely alter our duties and obligations'.[1]

From this we must conclude that in the sections concerned with the artificial virtues Hume advances arguments which commit him to the view that there can be practical judgements about the necessity of adopting the means in view of the desired end. We do not merely judge that respecting the property of others is a means to conserving our own, but also that in view of this fact we are obliged to or must respect their property. And this is a practical judgement. Hence, in these sections, Hume both makes more explicit and develops his theory of the practical influence of directive judgement, but this development is in no way contrary to his general position. For, even in so far as he admits that by making judgements we can formulate rules of conduct, and hence, that there are certain judgements capable of being made whose effect is essential to them, he in no way implies that reason and judgement are more than the *mediate cause* of action. For although these judgements, by their very nature, must affect the desires of those agents who make them and consider them true of themselves, yet their truth, and hence their efficacy, depend on a pre-existing desire. We cannot judge that on reflection we must be moved by the thought of $y$ because $y$ is a means to $x$ which is desired, unless we reflect, and in reflecting, actually come into this state. It is the process of judging prior to the concluding judgement which raises in us this desire. But such judging would not have this effect if, on reflection, $y$ did not prove to be desirable in view of some pre-existing desire $x$

[1] *Treatise*, ii, p. 200.

by being the condition without which $x$ could not be fulfilled; and if $y$ did not prove to be desirable, no concluding judgement about the necessity or obligation to do $y$ could be made. The understanding here, as Hume rightly says, does not create new desires; what it does is to 'control the interested affection' by 'an alteration of its direction'. The restraint imposed by it is not 'contrary to these passions', but only 'contrary to their heedless and impetuous movement'.

We have said that Hume's account of the directive functions of judgement is considerably enlarged in the doctrine of the artificial virtues. None the less he overlooks certain points which we must consider if our examination of this account is to be complete.

First it is evident that he did not see that his earlier exposition of this influence stood in need of certain amendments. As the result of his arguments here, he should have admitted the possibility of demonstrative practical judgements inferred from empirical premises. For it is plain that the judgements whereby we conclude that we have natural obligations involve precisely those mental processes which we discussed at the end of the last chapter. These are judgements which draw the conclusion from an inquiry directed to discovering the connexions between already existing desires and that which is implied by them, or is an instance of them. All practical judgements which direct passions are of this kind. If Hume had recognized this point, he would have had to modify substantially his earlier views on the relation between demonstrative reasoning and conduct.

Secondly, as the result of his arguments here, Hume should have admitted that there is a 'third error which can enter into our reasoning concerning action'. For we may fail to do certain actions not merely because we fail to realize that they are a means to a desired end, but because we fail to realize that in view of this fact these actions must be done. The admission of this 'third error' would have invalidated those of Hume's arguments in the earlier sections which imply that judgements which are merely the mediate causes of action cannot be the foundation of moral conduct. It is true that judgements which assert merely that $x$ is a means to $y$ are judgements of external fact, and, as Hume says, cannot be the source of morality or immorality. But judgements about the necessity of doing certain acts which are means to ends are of a different kind. These judgements, as Hume himself points out, give rise to a 'kind' of obligation. And, even though we do not have to maintain that when we act in accordance with them we as yet act morally and when we fail to do so we act immorally, yet it is clear that the influence of such judgements is precisely that kind of influence which is normally attributed also to moral judgements. These judgements exhibit imperatives, if only hypothetical ones; they are concerned not with the *possibility* of doing certain actions, but with some practical *necessity* of doing them. They impose *obligations* to which Hume later refers as a 'species of morality'.[1]

Thirdly, we must again call attention to a point which we noted in the beginning of the present chapter, namely, that Hume is mistaken in confining judgements which direct passions to those which are concerned with means to ends. Judgements about the nature of objects can also direct passions where the characteristics which these judgements attribute to them are already desired. In this case also it is evident that there can be both theoretical and practical directive judgements.[2] The rules which result from directive judgement cannot be confined to rules concerned with the necessity of adopting means.

Fourthly, there is an important distinction which Hume fails to draw, that is the distinction between the making of false directive judgements and the failure to make such judgements at all. According to the theory he advances in the earlier sections our conduct can only be said to be unreasonable when it results from the making of false judgements. I act unreasonably when I am mediately determined by the judgement that this train will take me to London and when this judgement is false. But this is not the conclusion we should draw from his

---

[1] *Treatise*, ii, p. 267.          [2] See above, p. 103.

doctrine of the artificial virtues, which would lead me to conclude that the unreasonableness of conduct results rather from a failure to determine our conduct by such judgements than from its determination by false ones. Our unreasonable actions, Hume here seems to imply, are those which result from passions alone, passions which are 'blind' and 'without the direction of [reason]', and which move us 'heedlessly and impetuously'. Our acts are called unreasonable not when we make false judgements about how to acquire property, but when we merely seize the goods of others, without making any judgement about what it is necessary for us to do if we want to acquire them. Thus, on this ground too, Hume's earlier view stands in need of amendment. And indeed the second view seems far more plausible than the first. We do normally think that an unreasonable action is one which is done entirely without reflection and forethought, and that if a man has reflected about his actions and they are caused by this reflection he has acted reasonably even though his reasoning was fallacious. For he has then been determined by his rational faculty even though the operation of this faculty in this case proved imperfect, and to do more than this was not within his power.

Hume's argument might have been elaborated and made more consistent if he had taken these four points into consideration, but it is plain that they would not have affected his basic view.

We must now turn to our second problem, namely how would Hume have answered the question: Can we make practical judgements which prompt passions, i.e. judgements about what it would be necessary for us to do on reflection in view of the intrinsic nature of the actions open to us and our own instinctive dispositions?

Now there is no doubt that Hume never explicitly asks himself this question, and in order to discover what attitude towards it is implicit in the *Treatise* it will be best first to consider briefly what such judgements would be like.

It is, I think, a matter of common experience that we do

continually make judgements of this kind. We make them whenever we ask ourselves the question which can be formulated most briefly as 'Do I really want to do $x$?' or more adequately as: 'Are the qualities of $x$ such that, if I were to consider them attentively, that is, to the exclusion of anything else, for some considerable time, I should either continue to desire $x$ or come into a state of desiring $x$?' Or, 'Is my desire for $x$ such that it could not be affected by any further reflection about the nature of $x$, its intrinsic and relational characteristics?' We do, in fact, try to answer questions of this kind, and when we do so our answer is always a practical judgement. It is not a judgement of the form '$x$ has the property $a$', or '$x$ has the property $b$', but of the form 'since $x$ has the properties $a\ b\ c\ \ldots$ I must, on contemplating the fact that it has these properties, desire to do it'. Conduct which is regulated by judgements of this kind is essentially different from conduct which is regulated by their theoretical counterparts alone. For, as we have already seen, judgements about the nature of objects and actions may fail to affect our desires altogether, or they may have a different effect from that which they would have if other conditions were fulfilled: that is, if further elucidatory judgements were made, if the ideas resulting from these judgements were before the mind for a longer period, and if they were before it to the exclusion of other ideas. Moreover, we have said that judgements about the nature of *objects* will not have any effect until they are connected with the ideas of *actions*, and judgements about the nature of *actions* will have no effect until they are connected with ideas of *my actions*. Now it is evident that in cases where we do not inquire whether a certain action would be an object of desire on reflection, or whether an object is of such a kind that some actions connected with it would be desired on reflection, these further conditions may well remain unfulfilled. Often they will in fact not be fulfilled but, more essentially, whether they are fulfilled or not will depend on chance alone. In such circumstances my conduct will in all probability be different from what it would have been if I had reflected. It is true, indeed, that the process of inquiring and of making a practical judgement may also not result in the total fulfilment of all these conditions, for I may still fail to make that number of elucidatory judgements needed in order for an idea to affect my conduct in the way in which it would affect it if I fully understood its nature. But by making such an inquiry I at least do my best to ensure that this is so. I allow my theoretical judgements about the nature of actions and objects to have the full effect of which they are capable. We have said already that theoretical judgements may have this same effect as the result not of some further judgement, but of association, but whether we happen to have the right associations is purely fortuitous. It is only by entering upon a specific inquiry about the way in which such judgements must, on reflection, affect us in given circumstances, that we can get any assurance that they will have this effect—it is only then that we act in the belief that our action is what we really desire.[1]

We can conclude that there are practical judgements which prompt passions, and that these judgements play an important part in the determination of our conduct. We have now to ask whether Hume makes allowance for them. This is a question which it is not easy to answer. We have already remarked that he nowhere explicitly draws the distinction between theoretical and practical judgements, and the absence of this dis-

---

[1] It may perhaps be granted that our theoretical judgements do not usually have the full effect of which they are capable until we have entered upon an inquiry aimed at discovering what effect is proper to them. Yet it may be argued that this inquiry need not terminate in a judgement. For will it not be the case that as soon as we have made the necessary further theoretical judgements and entertained the idea which we form as the result of them for a certain period they will have an effect without any specific answer to our enquiry being made? When we have done these things, it may be said, the actual answering of the question can serve no further purpose, for have not all the conditions which could arouse desire already been fulfilled? But in answer to this we must point out that there are psychological reasons why, once I have asked myself the question: 'Do I really want to do x?' and so long as the idea of asking myself this question remains before my mind, I will feel unready to do x until my question has been answered. For the doubt which is raised by this question acts as an inhibiting factor until the question has received a definite answer in propositional form. I shall be affected by my inquiring, but my being so affected will prove abortive, that is to say it will not lead to a settled readiness to act, until I have concluded my inquiry with the judgement that x is the proper object of desire for me.

tinction is more marked in the case of promptive than in that of directive ones. He does allow that there are laws or rules about what we must do in view of a given end, but he never admits that we form such rules about what acts should become our ends. It is true that in the earlier sections where he first mentions the judgements which prompt actions he refers to these judgements as concerned with the 'proper objects' of our desire;[1] but he does not say that these judgements are of the form *that* something is the proper object of desire, that is, that it must be done, but merely that they are *about* the proper object of our desire; and if we take this in conjunction with his examples we see that he is referring here only to judgements of the form '*x* is of the kind *y*' in cases where the thought of a thing of the kind *y* does in fact raise desire. Nevertheless, the problem of practical promptive judgements did not altogether elude Hume's attention.

This becomes plain when we turn to the sections on the 'calm' and 'violent' passions together with those later passages where Hume refers back to these sections. The whole distinction between the calm and the violent passions is of the greatest interest for our general problem, for it is introduced by Hume in order to explain what we 'really' mean when we talk about reasonable conduct. The doctrine of the calm passions is advanced as an alternative to rationalism. We shall consider this doctrine in detail in the next chapter, and we shall see there that it is exceedingly complex and does not allow of any simple interpretation; for Hume says so many different things about the calm passions that we must conclude either that he attributes several meanings to this term or that he thinks passions can be 'calm' in more ways than one. Here we are concerned only with one sense in which the term is used, or one way in which a passion can be calm, namely, that which Hume describes by saying that it is a passion 'founded on a distant view or reflection'.[2]

[1] *Treatise*, ii, p. 168: '. . . reason . . . can have an influence on our conduct . . . when it excites a passion, by informing us of the existence of something which is a proper object of it. . . .'
[2] Ibid., p. 279.

Now to be determined as the result of such reflection is in fact, according to Hume, to be determined by an adequate idea. Men act from a violent passion when they 'proportion their affections more to the light under which any object appears to them, than to its *real and intrinsic value*',[1] when they do not give preference 'to what is *in itself* preferable',[2] or when they expect from any object more pleasure or pain 'than what, strictly speaking, naturally belongs to it'.[3] In all these passages Hume is concerned with the difference between being determined by an idea which is adequate to its object, and being determined by an idea which results only from the particular way in which we view its object. Indeed the greater part of the sections on the 'calm' and 'violent' passions consists of a description of the ways in which we come to be moved by inadequate ideas, the ways in which ideas acquire more force than what, strictly speaking, properly belongs to them. That they acquire such force is always due to the peculiar situation of the agent who forms them: 'All depends', Hume writes, 'on the situation of the object [in relation to the agent]; a variation in this particular will be able to change the calm and violent passions into each other.'[4]

The circumstances in which we form an inadequate idea of an action or of one action compared with another are very many. We desire to do actions, for instance, simply because they are forbidden, for we find their relation to us in being forbidden attractive and when we desire them on this account it is their appearance to us, *qua* being forbidden, which makes us desire them, and we disregard their other qualities; '. . . we naturally desire what is forbid, and take a pleasure in performing actions, merely because they are unlawful'.[5] Again, we are attracted to do some acts because we are familiar with them[6] and can do them easily, and conversely we are attracted to do others because we are unfamiliar with them; 'everything that is new is most affecting, and gives us either more pleasure or pain than

---

[1] Ibid., p. 235 (my italics).
[2] Ibid., p. 237 (my italics).
[3] Ibid., p. 134.
[4] Ibid., p. 130.
[5] Ibid., p. 132.
[6] Ibid., p. 133.

what, strictly speaking, naturally belongs to it'.[1] In all these
circumstances our own particular situation with regard to these
actions prevents us from forming adequate ideas of them. But
of all the circumstances which give rise to a distorted view of
the objects of our passions Hume lays most emphasis on those
which do so through the medium of our imagination, and these
include our position in time and in space. It is evident, he
argues, that our ideas can be made lively by our imagination, which makes certain aspects of them unduly vivid or
makes certain ideas unduly vivid compared with other ideas.
'Wherever our ideas of good and evil acquire a new vivacity, the passions become more violent, and keep pace with
the imagination in all its variations.'[2] It is thus that:

> 'Any pleasure with which we are acquainted, affects us more than
> any other which we own to be superior, but of whose nature we are
> wholly ignorant. Of the one we can form a particular and determinate
> idea: the other we conceive under the general notion of pleasure; and
> it is certain that the more general and universal any of our ideas are, the
> less influence they have upon the imagination.'[3]

Again, Hume argues that when we have recently performed
some act our idea of this act is disproportionately vivid to those
of its alternatives 'of which the traces are decayed, and almost
obliterated'.[4] And again, that we are affected more by the ideas
of pleasures which are suitable to our way of life than those
which are foreign to it.[4] But his most elaborate statements
about the causes of these inadequate ideas are concerned with
the effects on the imagination of contiguity and distance in time
and space. Our position in time and space always affects our
imaginative conception of any action:

> 'There is an easy reason why everything contiguous to us, either in
> space or time, should be conceived with a peculiar force and vivacity,
> and excel every other object in its influence on the imagination. Ourself
> is intimately present to us, and whatever is related to self must partake

---

[1] *Treatise*, ii, p. 134.

[2] Ibid., p. 135. It is evident that a vivacious idea is not the same as an
adequate one. The idea of a certain act may occupy the mind to the exclusion
of other ideas and yet be far from adequate, for this idea may only incorporate
a few qualities of its object.

[3] Ibid.                                               [4] Ibid., p. 137.

of that quality. . . . It is obvious that the imagination can never totally forget the points of space and time in which we are existent; but receives such frequent advertisement of them from the passions and senses, that, however it may turn its attention to foreign and remote objects, it is necessitated every moment to reflect on the present.'[1]

Since the imagination is affected by proximity in time and space and thus distorts our ideas, Hume argues that our passions must be similarly distorted:

'If my reasoning be just, [time and space] must have a proportionable effect on the will and passions. Contiguous objects must have an influence much superior to the distant and remote.'[2]

Objects which are remote 'by reason of the interruption in our manner of conceiving them, appear in a weaker and more imperfect light';[2] 'distance weakens the conception and passion'.[3]

Now, inasmuch as Hume allows that there are calm passions which are founded on a 'distant view and reflection', he really should admit also that we can make practical promptive judgements. For to found a passion on a distant view or reflection, in this sense, is precisely the same as to found it on judgements which we make as the result of inquiring whether it is the sort of passion which we should have if we were to form an adequate idea of its object. It is true, of course, that a passion may be 'founded on a distant view or reflection' without our so founding it. That is to say, we may reflect at random about the nature of an act without ever intending to discover whether this act is the kind of act we must want to do. But it would be very odd to maintain that while our desires can be founded on a

---

[1] Ibid., p. 138.       [2] Ibid., p. 139.

[3] Ibid., p. 142. It is interesting to compare these passages with certain propositions in Spinoza's *Ethics*. We find arguments very similar to Hume's which are concerned with space and time in Part IV, the Scholium to Prop. IX, and in Prop. X, XI, XII, and XIII. Moreover, Hume and Spinoza both use these arguments as an explanation of how we can desire our own lesser good. See Hume's section 'Of Government' and the *Ethics*, Part IV, Scholium to Prop. XVII. Men, according to Spinoza, are more often moved by opinion than by true reason; and Hume argues that 'men are mightily governed by the imagination, and proportion their affections more to the light under which any object appears to them, than to its real and intrinsic value'. See also the Scholium to Prop. LXII, *Ethics*, Part IV, where Spinoza describes the distorting effects on the passions of the imagination whereby we form ideas of future things.

distant view or reflection, their being so founded is always a matter of accident and is never brought about intentionally. Nor does Hume in fact contend that this is the case. He argues that although we are often governed by violent passions, yet 'the calm ones, *when corroborated by reflection, and seconded by resolution,* are able to control them in their most furious movements'.[1] The reflection which corroborates calm passions must be concerned with whether these passions are the passions which we must really have on reflection; and the resolution which seconds them must constitute a principle of action which we form as the result of this 'reflection', a principle similar to the means-ends imperatives which Hume allows with regard to justice. It is true indeed that Hume does not place much confidence in these judgements. Either he thinks that they are not often made, or else that normally they are forgotten as soon as they are made and before they have time to take effect. Our adequate ideas vanish and those of the imagination reassert themselves: 'Men are not able radically to cure, that narrowness of soul . . . which makes them prefer the present to the remote.'[2] But in saying that they are not able 'radically' to cure it, he implies that they can do so in some degree. It is true Hume's whole theory of government is based on the observation that this 'narrowness of soul' cannot be wholly cured,[3] yet what is of

---

[1] *Treatise*, ii, p. 147 (my italics).    [2] Ibid., p. 238.

[3] Hume's argument here is very interesting, though it is but a new form of an argument that was common in the seventeenth century. Men, he argues, agree to submit to government because they cannot sufficiently succeed in making the calm passions prevail over the violent. At any given time they are moved by the thought of what is conducive to their present well-being, rather than what would be conducive to their greatest well-being in the future. For their imagination prevents them from forming adequate ideas of both these well-beings, and always prejudices them in favour of the present. This difficulty is, according to Hume, overcome because, when both acts are in the distant future, we see them as they really are, and 'give preference to what is in itself preferable'. We then, by a kind of trick on ourselves, make arrangements so that that which we desire when they are both distant will also be the one which we desire when one is near. We do this by arranging to be punished for doing that which we desired least when both were distant, and in this way make this appear as the lesser good to our imagination as well as to our reflection. We arrange things, that is to say, so that we act *as though* our ideas were adequate even when they are not.·

This argument has a certain special interest for us. For here we find some link between the influence of judgements about means to ends and the influence of those about the nature of objects. We make judgements about the nature

interest for our purpose is his admission that our actions, when we fail to cure it, are unreasonable. For he not only refers to our tendency to be moved by inadequate ideas as a 'narrowness of soul' and a 'natural infirmity',[1] but he remarks that it leads to 'fatal errors' in conduct: 'There is no quality in human nature', he writes, 'which causes more fatal errors in our conduct, than that which leads us to prefer whatever is present to the distant and remote, and makes us desire objects more according to their situation than their intrinsic value.'[2] In making this statement Hume is admitting that the unreasonableness of acts can be due to our failure to make judgements about what acts must be done, or are proper objects of desire. Acting from inadequate ideas, preferring what is not in itself preferable, is here described by him as an 'error' in conduct. This error lies not in the fact that our acts result from false judgements about the nature of actions, but in our failure to reflect about what acts are really preferable, or in our failure to make a correct judgement as the result of such reflection. For giving preference to what is not in itself preferable, preferring the present to the remote, can only be defined in terms of preferring that which we would not prefer were we to think about its object more adequately. It is being moved to do that which we would not be moved to do if we were to consider what we must be moved to do.[3]

Thus in this case also we have to say that Hume makes some allowance for practical judgements. It is true that the passages from which we can conclude that he would have allowed for such judgements if he had considered them explicitly are more

of our future well-being and the acts which must now be done or avoided as the means to attaining it. But if our idea of future well-being is less adequate than that of our present well-being, which in fact, is less, then we shall do $x$, which is constitutive of our present well-being, rather than $y$, which is a means to greater well-being in the future.

[1] Ibid., p. 235.            [2] Ibid., p. 239.

[3] The view that Hume does to some extent, at least implicitly, allow that there can be practical judgements which prompt actions receives considerable support if we compare his calm passions doctrine with his theory of valuations. The two doctrines present an interesting parallel with the one difference that in the second case Hume argues that *all* values are dependent upon judgements about what must be approved of on reflection. See below, Chapter VI.

scattered and less unequivocal than those from which we concluded that he would have to allow for practical directive judgements. None the less they provide us with a ground for saying that the admission of such judgements was implicit in the *Treatise*, and that his other arguments needed such an admission if they were to be complete. The views that there are theoretical judgements which direct passions and that there are theoretical judgements which prompt passions are not complete unless we allow that there are also practical judgements with both these functions.

With these remarks we have come to the end of our analysis of Hume's account of the influence which empirical and *a priori* judgements can have on action. We can now sum up our conclusions about what powers he granted and what he withheld. Our general conclusion is that he does in fact allow, both explicitly and implicitly, a far greater power to reason than is often supposed. He makes it perfectly plain that theoretical judgements both empirical and *a priori* have a very great influence on action, and that this influence is a common one which partakes in the determining, if not of all, yet at least of a great many acts: 'Human nature' is 'composed of two principle parts which are requisite in all its actions, the affections and understanding',[1] and the affections unaided by the understanding are 'blind'. Moreover, we have seen that his admission that these theoretical judgements influence action drives him towards admitting also that there are practical judgements of the same kinds, judgements which are the foundation of our 'natural obligations'. We have not argued that the admission of these judgements is explicit in the *Treatise*, only that it is implicit, but our interpretation may be an unnecessarily guarded one. We might be justified in regarding his assertion that as the result of making empirical judgements we form laws of conduct, not merely as implying that we make practical judgements about means to ends, but as actually being this assertion; and his remark that reflection and resolution sometimes enable us

[1] *Treatise*, ii, p. 198.

to control our violent passions, not as an assertion which implies that there are, but as itself the assertion that there are practical judgements which prompt action.

But extensive though these functions of reason are, it is plain that Hume could have allowed to reason still wider powers while remaining within the framework of his theory that reason is no more than the mediate cause of action. For all these functions are isolated from each other and each is limited in scope. All that Hume ever considers are inquiries directed to finding (1) whether I must do $x$ since I desire $y$, and (2) whether I must do $x$ when I consider its intrinsic nature. He never considers at all inquiries which are directed towards discovering whether I must do $x$ rather than $y$ if I cannot do both; that is to say, he never considers choice, and the functions of reason in determining which of two possible actions must be desired.[1] It is for this reason also that all consideration of a wholly comprehensive practical judgement is omitted from the *Treatise*. Hume never considers the possibility of our asking not: 'Must I do $x$?' but: 'Of all acts which are possible in this situation which must I do?' The answer to this question would be a comprehensive practical judgement. For in order to answer it we would have to inquire: (1) What acts are possible in the situation; (2) Which of these acts are such that they are in themselves desirable; (3) Which act is more desirable than all its alternatives; (4) Which acts are desirable as a means to this end; and (5) Are these means in themselves so undesirable that in view of them some other alternative would be a preferable end? The complexity of the functions of reason where we try to answer a comprehensive question of this kind is clearly very great, and Hume was far from realizing the full complexity of the judgements which can in fact influence action.

[1] It is true of course that in the section 'Of Government' (see footnote to p. 136), as elsewhere, he does consider what we do in a situation where we are faced with the possibility of doing one act which is constitutive of our present well-being or another act which is a means to a state which is constitutive of our future well-being. But I think we are justified in saying that in this case there is no choice, for it is well-being which is desired, and the problem is only one of forming adequate ideas of which act will do the most to promote 'our greatest possible good'.

# CHAPTER V

## REASON THE SLAVE OF THE PASSIONS

IT is commonly thought that the most outstanding single point which Hume makes in the second and third books of the *Treatise* is his denial that the ways in which reason can influence action have any very considerable importance or interest, and his consequent rejection of the common seventeenth- and eighteenth-century view that reason and judgement play the central part in our moral and practical life. No such conclusion can be drawn from those arguments we have so far discussed. But there are many passages which support this view and they are worded in no dubious terms: 'reason', Hume asserts, 'is perfectly inert';[1] 'it is, and ought only to be, the slave of the passions';[2] it cannot 'ever keep the mind in suspense a moment'.[2] Moreover, he argues that when we think we are governed by reason we are in fact ruled by a passion which only 'feels' like reason.[3] That is to say, he actually goes so far as to argue that there is a phenomenon which is taken for rational motivation, but mistakenly so.

Thus it seems as though we are faced with two contradictory doctrines. On the one hand, Hume maintains that 'the understanding is requisite in all our actions' on the other that 'reason is perfectly inert'. We have now to examine the second of these theories and, having done so, to inquire how far it is really incompatible with the former. Only then shall we be in a position to say what powers Hume allotted to reason, all things considered, and how far such restrictions as he places on this power are the essential consequence of his views on the relation of reason and action, and how far they are due to extraneous causes and might be abandoned without detriment to his general position.

Our first task in the present chapter then is to examine those arguments where Hume does most to discredit reason and ex-

---

[1] *Treatise*, ii, p. 167.  [2] Ibid., p. 127.
[3] Ibid., p. 128.

plain away the common belief that reason does have a significant effect on our conduct. These arguments form two doctrines which are closely connected and are, in parts, overlapping. The first is that when we think we are moved by reason we are in fact moved by a special kind of passion which Hume calls a 'calm passion'; the second that reason is operative only as the 'slave of the passions'. We shall begin by considering the first, and we shall find that this consideration naturally leads us to examine the second also.

Here first we must note that the 'calm passions' doctrine is exceedingly difficult to understand. It is neither so coherently stated nor so carefully elaborated as most of Hume's other arguments. Certain of his remarks about the nature of the distinction between the calm and violent passions seem to conflict with others. Indeed, it is so difficult to produce conclusive evidence for any one interpretation of this theory that I should hesitate to offer any, if some were not necessary for any attempt to understand his more negative attitude towards the power of reason.

Now Hume devotes several whole sections to the calm and violent passions, and in these sections, and later where he refers back to them, he seems to describe these passions in five different ways. (i) He remarks that the calm passions 'produce little emotion in the mind', and like reason they 'scarce ever convey any pleasure or uneasiness'.[1] (ii) He divides the calm passions into two kinds; they are 'either certain instincts originally implanted in our natures, such as benevolence and resentment, the love of life, and kindness to children; or the general appetite to good, and aversion to evil, considered merely as such'.[1] It is evident, however, that this description is not intended to be a complete one, for he adds that these passions are calm 'when' they are calm: 'when any of these passions are calm, and cause no disorder in the soul, they are very readily taken for the determination of reason.'[1] Moreover, he goes on to remark that passions of these 'same kinds' may also be violent: 'Besides these calm passions, which often determine

[1] Ibid., p. 129.

the will, there are certain violent emotions *of the same kind.*'[1]
From this it follows that we cannot take the above list of calm
passions as a definition by enumeration. That $x$ is a passion
given in Hume's list does not entail that $x$ is calm; and yet the
list has evidently some significance in Hume's distinction.
(iii) There are passages where Hume implies that to be determined by a calm passion is to be motivated by the thought of
that act which we conceive to be conducive to our 'greatest
possible good'. In speaking of the calm and violent passions
he remarks that 'men often act knowingly against their interest;
for which reason, the view of the greatest possible good does
not always determine them', and he adds that 'Men often
counteract a violent passion in prosecution of their interests
and designs; it is not, therefore, the present uneasiness alone
which determines them.'[2] (iv) There are passages where he
says that to be determined by a calm passion is to be determined
according to the 'real and intrinsic value' of an object and not
merely by the 'light under which [it] appears to [us]'.[3] It is to
give 'preference to whatever is in itself preferable',[3] or to be
determined by a 'distant view or reflection'.[4] (v) Hume argues
that to be determined by a calm passion is to be determined
by 'a settled principle of action' or 'the predominant inclination
of the soul'.[5]

If we are to understand Hume's calm-passions doctrine we
have to take all these statements into account. It is not easy
to see how they are connected, but we must endeavour to find
some relation between them. First we may note his remark
that the calm passions, unlike the violent, are 'accompanied by
little sensible emotion'. Here he is drawing between these passions the kind of distinction which he is very fond of drawing.
It is on similar lines that he distinguishes between ideas and
impressions, impressions differing from ideas in feeling quality
by having a greater vivacity. But it is plain that this distinction
in terms of feeling quality is not supposed to be the fundamental one. Evidently it is only symptomatic of some more

---

[1] *Treatise*, ii, p. 129 (my italics).    [2] Ibid.    [3] Ibid., p. 235.
[4] Ibid., p. 279.                          [5] Ibid., p. 130.

fundamental difference which is constitutive of the difference between calmness and violence. We can also leave aside for the time being the distinction which he makes by enumerating which passions are calm and which are violent, for, as we have seen, he says that the 'same' passions can be either calm or violent. We are then left with passages of three kinds: those according to which the calm passions are caused by the thought of our 'greatest possible good'; those according to which they are in accordance with the 'intrinsic value' of their objects; and those according to which they are 'settled principles' or 'predominant inclinations of the soul'. Of these three it is the second on which Hume lays the greatest stress, but the other two are, as we shall see, closely connected with it.

We have already discussed this second description of the calm passions at some length in the last chapter. There is no need to say much about it here. We need only recall that to be moved by a calm passion in this sense is to be moved by the thought of an act which is 'in itself preferable', by a passion which accords with the 'real and intrinsic value' of its object.[1] But in the light of this view, several of Hume's other remarks can be understood. From Hume's arguments as a whole it is possible to deduce that he thought that desires which are calm in this sense can be caused in either of two ways. They can arise, on the one hand, in the way which we have described in the last chapter, that is as the result of our actually forming adequate ideas of their objects by making a series of theoretical judgements. On the other hand, they can arise quite fortuitously without any adequate idea ever being entertained. For we may, by nature or by upbringing, be so disposed that, without any express attempt to do so, we in fact have those desires which we should have if we had formed and entertained adequate ideas of their objects. This case can, I think, best be described by saying that our passions are *materially* calm without being *formally* so. They are calm because they happen to be directed towards those objects towards which they would be directed

[1] See above, Chapter IV, pp. 132 ff.

*if* we considered these objects adequately. Hence they have the *matter* or *content* of a calm passion. But they have not the *form* of such a passion because they do not in fact arise from any such idea. That Hume regarded our calm passions as sometimes both materially and formally calm is evident from his remark that they are 'founded on some distant view or reflection',[1] and that our conduct is determined by such passions when they are 'corroborated by reflection and seconded by resolution'. On the other hand, it follows from his remarks about 'settled dispositions' and 'predominant inclinations of the soul' that he did regard the calm passions as sometimes calm in a material sense alone. We will return to the problem of the ways in which passions can become calm when we consider the relation between determination by these calm passions and determination by reason. Here we need only note that in so far as Hume thought that a calm passion is a passion which accords with the intrinsic value of its object we have already one explanation of his description of calm passions in terms of their feeling quality. For it is plain that passions which are firmly rooted in the nature of their objects will have persistence. They will not be at the mercy of every new discovery about their object. Hence they are likely to feel calm and undisturbing, while those which are not so rooted and are liable to new variations every time some new fact about their object is noted will, by their constant fluctuations, cause what Hume calls 'a disturbance in the soul'.

We can then conclude that Hume's view of the calm passions as those whereby we give 'preference to what is in itself preferable' is closely related to and accounts for his remarks both that these passions are 'founded on a distant view or reflection' and that they spring from 'settled dispositions' or 'the predominant inclination of the soul'. And, further, that this, at least in part, explains his description of these passions in terms of feeling quality. Thus there remains to be accounted for only those passages where Hume seems to identify calm passions as passions which are conducive to 'our greatest possible good', and

[1] *Treatise*, ii, p. 279.

those where he specifically enumerates these passions which are sometimes calm and sometimes violent.

Here we have first to note that the passages where Hume says that the calm passions are those which are conducive to our 'greatest possible good' occur immediately after the passage where he enumerates what passions are calm and what are violent. Thus at the end of this enumeration he writes:

'The common error of metaphysicians has lain in ascribing the direction of the will entirely to one of these principles, [the calm and the violent], and supposing the other to have no influence. Men often act knowingly against their interest; for which reason, the view of the greatest possible good does not always influence them. Men often counteract a violent passion in prosecution of their own interests and designs; it is not, therefore, the present uneasiness alone which determines them. In general we may observe that both these principles operate on the will; and where they are contrary, that either of them prevails, according to the *general* character or *present* disposition of the person.'[1]

It is, I think, clear from this passage that Hume does regard a 'calm passion' as a desire to do an act which we think will be conducive to our 'greatest possible good'. It is a passion which is aroused on account of this end, one which is operative 'in prosecution of our interests or designs'. A violent passion, on the other hand, is merely a 'present uneasiness', an uneasiness which I feel 'independent of all considerations of pleasure and advantage to myself'.[1] A calm passion in this sense is a passion which is directed towards a state of affairs which I consider to be, of all those possible in the situation, that which will be most constitutive of my greatest possible good, or that which will lead to this state. A violent passion is one which is not related to my greatest possible good by being a passion either for a state constitutive of this good or for some means to this state. We can put this slightly differently by saying that a passion is calm when it is caused by an adequate idea of what will be constitutive of my greatest possible good in the present circumstances and what will lead to this; and that it is violent when it

[1] Ibid., p. 129.

is caused by an inadequate idea of this good and what will lead to it.

But if we attend to Hume's earlier passage where he enumerates the calm and violent passions, we shall have to conclude that he thought that a passion can be calm or violent by being related to good not in one but in two ways. It will be calm not merely when it is specifically aimed at achieving our good, but when it does so incidentally and without being so directed. For Hume evidently thinks that the 'certain instincts originally implanted in our nature, such as benevolence and resentment, the love of life and kindness to children' are calm when they do not conflict with the achievement of our general good, even though they are not directed to its achievement. For, in so far as they arise from instincts 'originally implanted in our nature', they are evidently independent of our desire for good. It is in this light that we must interpret the whole passage where Hume argues that the calm desires are 'of two kinds': instincts implanted in our nature and 'the general appetite to good, and aversion to evil, considered merely as such', and then proceeds to argue that these same desires can also be violent. These desires are calm when they are conducive to the greatest possible good and violent when they conflict with it. There remains, however, one point which we must consider in this connexion. For it appears from the above that Hume is saying that the 'desire for good and aversion to evil considered merely as such' can itself at times be a calm and at others a violent desire. Such a statement is, at least prima facie, exceedingly odd; for if a calm passion is defined, as it evidently is in the subsequent paragraph, as a passion conducive to good, then clearly the desire for good itself must always be calm. There are, however, two possible explanations. The one is that in enumerating the violent passions Hume simply overlooked the fact that he had included the desire for good in his list of the calm ones, and that in saying that the violent passions were 'of the same kind' he did not mean to include under the 'same kind' the desire for good itself. But, I think, the more plausible explanation is that Hume drew a distinction between the desire for *good* and the desire for the *greatest possible good*; and that he thought of passions as calm and violent in relation only to the latter. In so far as this is so we need not deny that the desire for some particular good or well-being may be a violent passion. Our desire for that which is constitutive of our present good may well be prejudicial to our greatest possible good. That this is Hume's view is supported by his remarks in the section 'Of Government', where he speaks of man having an 'inclination to present good' which he calls 'a violent propension to prefer the present to the remote'.[1]

This view of the calm passions like that which we have discussed above also justifies the further distinction between the calm and violent passions in terms of feeling quality. For it is evident that when passions are calm in the sense that they are either conducive to or directed towards our greatest possible good they are co-ordinated with one another and cannot come into conflict. Such passions, since they do not conflict, cause no disorder in the soul, for it is only when our passions are not co-ordinated by a single principle that they can cause a 'sensible emotion'.

We have now given some account of all those remarks about the calm and violent passions which we enumerated at the beginning. We can sum up by saying that Hume held two views of the distinction between these passions, or rather that he thought this distinction could be drawn on two grounds— for these two views are not strictly alternatives but are complementary. A passion is calm either when it is a passion whereby we give preference to 'what is in itself preferable' or when it is a passion for what is preferable considered as constitutive of or conducive to our greatest possible good. It is violent either when we give preference to what is not in itself preferable or to what is not preferable when considered as constitutive of or conducive to happiness or well-being. In either case, the calmness of the passion is dependent on its conformity with the real and not the imaginary qualities of its object, in the first on these qualities as they are in themselves, in the second on their

[1] See above, Ch. IV, p. 136, n. 3.

relation to the agent's well-being. It seems true to say that Hume did not draw the distinction between these two kinds of calm passion very clearly, yet there can be no doubt that he did regard passions as susceptible to both kinds of calmness. His other remarks all fall into place if we consider them as indicative of the ways in which passions can become calm in both these senses. For our desires can become calm in either sense *either* when we consider the intrinsic qualities of their objects or their relation to happiness and form an adequate idea of these qualities or this relation, *or* when it so happens that these desires are of themselves the kind of desires which would result from such a consideration. Here again we cannot say that Hume explicitly distinguishes these two ways in which passions can become calm, but again it is difficult to interpret his remarks in any other way and still retain a coherent theory.

Having offered some analysis of the calm-passions doctrine we are now in the position to consider the relation of this doctrine to Hume's views on practical reason. We have seen that he advances this doctrine as an alternative to rationalism. When we think we are determined by reason, he argues, we are in fact determined by a calm passion. We have now to inquire in what sense being determined by a calm passion really is an alternative to being determined by reason. According to our interpretation of this doctrine we are determined by a calm passion when the thought of an object affects us in the way in which it would affect us *either* if we had an adequate idea of its qualities as they are in themselves *or* if we had an adequate idea of these qualities in relation to our happiness. In discussing this doctrine in relation to the influence of reason on conduct we shall have to consider these two cases separately. But we have seen also that we must conclude from Hume's remarks that passions which are calm in either way can be caused either by a 'distant view or reflection' or fortuitously because our dispositions and education have made us the kind of person who does what he would do if he reflected. This distinction of the two ways in which calm passions can arise is of the utmost importance for the relation of the calm-passions doctrine to rationalism. Indeed for our present purpose it is best to consider the calm passions as being of four kinds: (i) Desires which accord with the real qualities of their objects independently of a special consideration of these objects. (ii) Desires which accord with these qualities as the result of the agent forming an adequate conception of them. (iii) Desires which accord with the real qualities of their objects as constitutive of or a means to happiness without the agent considering them as such. (iv) Desires which accord with these qualities as constitutive of or a means to happiness as the result of the agent forming an adequate idea of them in this relation.

Now, it is plain that where calm passions are of the first and the third kinds, they are wholly independent of reason and judgement, and determination by them is genuinely an alternative to determination by judgement. In both these cases we are determined *as though* by reason and judgement: our passions are durable and are well co-ordinated, our actions are those of a reasonable man. Yet in neither case does reason play any part in their determination. The principle by which we are moved is, in fact, wholly conative, and operates without any intervention from our rational faculty. Moreover, Hume seems to be correct in saying that we are often moved in this way. We often desire from instinct or from habit those acts which in fact lead to our happiness, or which we should desire if we were to form an adequate idea of them. Our violent passions to do acts which are not of this kind are often subdued without the help of reason. A sudden impulse to steal is counteracted, not by a consideration of the nature and effects of stealing, but by a settled principle or permanent disposition not to steal. Impulses to kill, to throw ourselves from the top of the cliffs, to give up our jobs are usually counteracted in the same way. Moreover, Hume seems also to be right in thinking that we do confuse acting from desires which are caused in this way with acting reasonably. 'What we call strength of mind', he writes, 'implies the prevalence of the calm passions above the violent; though we may easily observe, there is no man so constantly possessed of this virtue as never on any occasion to yield to the solicitations of passion and desire.'[1] We do in fact say that people act reasonably when they do what they would have done if they had thought about it, or what will in fact lead to their happiness, and foolishly when they do what they would not have done if they had reflected, or what is in fact contrary to their interests. Whether they have in fact reflected or not is a question which we do not consider.

But if we turn to the calm passions of the second and fourth kinds it seems evident that being determined by these passions is not an alternative to being determined by reason at all. For these passions are themselves by definition determined by judgement. When we desire to do an act because we consider that it is constitutive of or a means to our greatest possible good, then we have a desire which is by definition mediately caused by the judgement that it is a means to or constitutive of good. Again, when a desire accords with what is in itself preferable because it is 'founded on a distant view or reflection', we have a desire which is dependent upon the judgement which results from this reflection. In the first case, we are motivated by a judgement about what kind of state of ourselves is constitutive of our greatest possible happiness where this happiness is already desired, or by a judgement about what will lead to this state. That is to say, our desires for particular actions are here caused by the kind of judgement which we have discussed in the last chapter, a judgement which 'directs' our passions. In the second case we are motivated by judgements about the nature of those actions which it is possible for us to do; that is to say, by judgements which 'prompt' passions. We can conclude that determination by calm passions of the second and fourth kind is not an alternative to determination by reason. Indeed determination by these calm passions is identical with the kind of rational determination which we have considered in the last two chapters, for these calm passions are precisely those which are directed and prompted by judgements.

[1] *Treatise*, ii, p. 130.

It seems then that although part of Hume's calm-passions doctrine does provide him with an alternative theory to rationalism, part of it does not. But I do not think we have to conclude from this that the calm-passions doctrine is ambiguous and contains within itself unsolved contradictions. If the interpretation which we have given to this doctrine is the correct one, then it seems likely that Hume did not at one time think of the calm passions as caused by a purely conative principle and at another as caused by a distant view or reflection, or the consideration of our greatest possible good, i.e. by judgement, but simply that he regarded them as capable of arising in the one and the other way. It would indeed be odd if this were not the case, for then Hume would not merely be putting forward two incompatible accounts of the calm passions, but one of these accounts would become altogether unintelligible. For it is not possible to explain what is meant by a calm passion which arises from a 'predominant inclination of the soul' without referring to those calm passions which are caused by 'a distant view or reflection'. The former are defined in terms of those passions which we should have if we reflected. But it would surely not be possible to maintain that there are passions which can only be defined in terms of those passions which we should have if we reflected, and at the same time deny that passions ever actually arise from reflection. We cannot contend both that reflection and judgement cannot cause action and that we can act as though we were caused to do so by reflection and judgement; for unless these processes can themselves cause action, then the descriptions of action in terms of 'as if caused by reflection and judgement' must be meaningless.

It seems then we must conclude that determination by calm passions is not on the whole the alternative to determination by reason which Hume intended it to be. From the arguments which we have considered it does not follow that whenever we are moved by a calm passion 'our reason is perfectly inert' or that it can never keep us 'in suspense a moment'. All that Hume seems to have argued is that though we are sometimes determined by a 'distant view or reflection' or a 'consideration of our own greatest possible good', yet at others when we appear to be determined in this way our passions are in fact only *as if* they were so determined. This is indeed a pertinent observation, but it seems to be only in the nature of a warning not to think that actions are caused by reason simply because we judge that they are the kind of actions that the agent would have done if he had reasoned, for such actions often occur without intervention from the understanding. It in no way bears out Hume's much more radical contention that what we believe to be rational determination is really determination by a special kind of passion.

Here then we seem to be faced with a dilemma. Is our interpretation of the calm-passions doctrine mistaken or inadequate? Or did Hume really not intend to say that when we are moved by a calm passion we are not moved by reason? It is difficult to answer this question, but I think that if we examine the calm-passions doctrine from another point of view we shall find that Hume is in fact justified in thinking that it has certain strikingly anti-rationalist implications. These implications are far more radical than those which can be drawn from the mere observation that sometimes when acts appear to be determined by reason they in fact only spring from settled dispositions and predominant inclinations of the soul.

In this connexion it is important to observe that the calm-passions doctrine occurs in close conjunction with Hume's assertion that '*reason is, and ought only to be, the slave of the passions*'. This assertion is immediately preceded by the re-mark that 'the principle which opposes our passion cannot be the same with reason, and is only called so in an improper sense'[1]—a clear reference to the calm passions—and Hume begins his discussion of these passions on the following page. The consideration of this fact throws new light on our problem, for it at once appears that Hume, in advancing the calm-passions doctrine, was not so much concerned with the power which judgements have over our actions once they are made, as with *how it is that we ever come to make them*. He is not

[1]    *Treatise*, ii, p. 127.

denying that actions can be mediately caused by reason; if reason could not affect our passions, there would, as we have seen, be no calm desires. What he is denying is that reason can ever come into operation as an *independent variable*.

Let us consider Hume's argument from this point of view. It is evident that his assertion that reason is the slave of the passions means that, although certain judgements may influence our conduct, they do so only in the service of other passions which are themselves beyond such rational control. Viewed in this light it seems that at least part of the calm-passions doctrine is a description of a particular case of this kind of determination. For all our desires which are calm, in the sense that they result from a consideration of our greatest possible happiness, ultimately depend not on our judgements about what acts will contribute most to this happiness, but on the desire for happiness which caused us to embark on the inquiry which terminated in these judgements. And this desire is one which Hume evidently does not consider as itself affected by any earlier judgement. Unfortunately Hume does not elaborate this theory, though it is of central importance for his whole conception of the relation between reason and action. But that he held such a view cannot be doubted. For first, it is the only possible interpretation of his statement that reason is the slave of the passions. Secondly, it follows logically from his view that reason is only the mediate cause of action. And thirdly, there are, as we have seen, no other grounds on which we can account for his ultimate rejection of rationalism, and his consistently depreciative attitude towards the practical power of reason and judgement. He grants that reason has considerable powers once it is operative, and his persistent remarks that these powers are ultimately a negligible factor in the control of our conduct can be attributed only to the view that reason is never operative as an independent variable, but that it is both brought into operation and guided in its operation by some passion which does not itself come under its control.

There is little we can add concerning the first of these points.

The assertion that reason is the slave of the passions must refer
to the fact that our reasoning is itself controlled by our passions; it cannot mean that reason when operating under the
control of one passion is powerless to control others, for that
it has this power Hume never denied. But the second and third
of these points must be considered further. Why, we must ask,
does the view that reason is the mediate cause of action entail
that it must always be brought into operation by a passion
which it cannot even mediately control? And how far does this
view justify Hume's ultimate rejection of the whole rationalist
position?

Let us begin by recalling what is meant by saying that reason
is the mediate cause of action. According to this view all actions are caused by desire, and all desires are caused by the
thought of the desired actions. All that reason can do in determining desires and actions is to acquaint us with facts which
will determine the nature of those ideas that are at any given
time before the mind. Now it is evident that this view about
the power of reason *when* it is operative implies a view about
the way in which reason can *come* into operation. For the
reasoning and judging by which we become acquainted with
the facts that modify our ideas of possible actions are themselves actions and as such they must also be determined by
desire.[1] It is true that this desire also may be mediately caused

---

[1] It is important to notice that in saying that reasoning and judging are
actions we are referring to the whole process of inquiry which terminates in
a judgement, and not to the judgement itself. It is evident that the actual
conclusion of an inquiry is not an action at all. I am not determined to draw
a certain conclusion from my accumulated evidence by the thought of doing so.
I do not draw what conclusion I will; the conclusion is forced upon me by the
evidence at hand. But the whole process of inquiry—seeking an answer to a
question, accumulating data, holding the data before the mind—what we may
call 'judging' as opposed to 'making a judgement'—is certainly an act.
    It must also be noted that in saying that judging is an act we are excluding
from judging certain processes which some might perhaps include under the
term, but I think mistakenly so. These processes might perhaps be called
'making observations'. They are more properly comprehended under 'perceiving'
than under 'judging'. But they acquaint us with facts which affect our conduct
in the same way as theoretical judgements. I may 'notice' that there are ripe
apples on this tree, or I may merely 'take in' another's assertion that this train
goes to London. Such perceptions or opinions can mediately affect our conduct,
but they do no result from inquiry and are not 'conclusions of our reason'.

by reasoning, but this reasoning in its turn must be caused by a passion, and, since all directed inquiries, being actions, are caused by passions, but not all passions are even mediately caused by reasoning, it follows that ultimately our inquiry is caused by a passion which is not controlled by reason and judgement in any sense. To illustrate this by an example. Let us assume that I desire to travel on the 10.20 from Oxford. This desire will in all probability mediately be caused by the judgement that the 10.20 goes to London. But my inquiry concerning the way to get to London must itself have been caused by the desire to make this inquiry. This in its turn was probably caused by the judgement that the way to be sure of getting to London is to inquire into the means of getting there. But this inquiry in its turn must have been caused by the desire to be sure of getting to London, which may indeed also have been caused by a judgement about the nature of being in London or the ends to which this was a means, but either this judgement or some other before it must have been caused by a desire which was totally independent of all reasoning. Whenever a desire is caused by a judgement, the inquiry which terminated in this judgement must have been caused by another desire, but this desire need not in its turn have been caused by another judgement. Thus in tracing the series of causes and effects backwards from any given desire we shall always find that this series terminates in a desire and not a judgement.

Now there can, I think, be no doubt that Hume's derogatory remarks about the practical power of reason are attributable to this view that the reasoning and judging which causes passions and actions is always itself caused by a passion. And yet we can still ask whether the slave-of-the-passions doctrine does really entail such a denial of the dignity of practical reason. Hume evidently took this view, but not all philosophers have concurred with him. Spinoza also thought that reason was no more than the mediate cause of action. All actions, he maintained, are caused by passions, and one passion can be counteracted only by another.[1] He also regarded reasoning and

[1] *Ethics*, Part IV, Prop. VII.

judging as actions and therefore as caused by passions. Yet Spinoza was very far from depreciating the control of reason over passions and actions in the way that Hume did; on the contrary, he regarded the power of controlling actions and passions by reason and judgement as that which differentiates man from beast and the free man from the slave:

'... we easily see the difference between the man who is led by emotion or opinion alone and the man who is led by reason. The former does willy nilly things which he knows absolutely nothing about; the latter, on the other hand, is governed only by himself and does only those things which he knows to be of primary importance for his life and which therefore he desires most. It is for this reason that I call the former a slave and the latter a free man.'[1]

Hence we have to ask whether, granted the slave-of-the-passions doctrine, we are also committed to Hume's depreciative view of practical reason, or whether we can yet conclude with Spinoza that practical reason is of central importance to man's life. If so, why did Hume fail to draw the same conclusion?

In answering this question it will be necessary to look for some variations between the slave-of-the-passions doctrine as it was held by Hume and as it was held by Spinoza which can account for the divergence of their views on the ultimate significance of practical reason. Now there is plainly one major variation to which the slave-of-the-passions doctrine is susceptible; for, granted we admit that reasoning is always caused by a passion, we may still take very different views about the kinds of passions which cause us to reason, and indeed in this respect Hume's view differs from Spinoza's very considerably. For Hume seems to have thought that the passion which prompts us to reason is always a passion for some particular end or for happiness. According to him, we desire to reason in order to discover the ways in which our other desires may be fulfilled, while Spinoza on the other hand maintains that we desire to reason for *its own sake*. Determining ourselves by reason is for Spinoza, as for Kant, an *end in itself*.[2] It is true

---

[1] *Ethics*, Scholium to Prop. LXVI. See also Proof of Prop. LXVII.
[2] It is interesting to notice that one of the eighteenth-century *a priori* moralists took a similar view. See John Balguy, *The Foundation of Moral Goodness*,

that Hume never specifically discusses this problem, so we cannot say he actually denies the possibility of such a desire, but there are no references to it anywhere in the *Treatise*, and it would be alien to the greater part of Hume's philosophy. The way in which reasoning comes into operation in the service of a desire for something else is, on the other hand, described in some detail:

'It is obvious, that when we have the prospect of pain or pleasure from any object, we feel a consequent emotion of aversity or propensity, and are carried to avoid or embrace what will give us this uneasiness or satisfaction. It is also obvious, that this emotion rests not here, but, making us cast our view on every side, comprehends whatever objects are connected with its original one by the relation of cause and effect. Here then reasoning takes place to discover this relation; and according as our reasoning varies, our actions receive a subsequent variation.'[1]

Moreover, as we have seen earlier in this chapter, Hume thought that our reasoning is very often made operative by the passion for our own greatest good. We reason and judge in order to discover what acts or states are constitutive of our true happiness, and what will lead to these. Turning to Spinoza we find a very different view. Spinoza constantly emphasizes that man desires to act rationally for the sake of so doing. He identifies rational and virtuous action, and of virtue he writes that it 'is to be desired for its own sake, nor is there anything more excellent or useful to us for the sake of which we ought to desire it',[2] and again:

'. . . the essence of reason is nothing other than our own mind in so far as it clearly and distinctly understands; hence that which I desire when governed by reason is nothing but to understand. And again, since this desire of the mind, whereby, in so far as it is reason, it desires to preserve its own essence, is nothing else but the desire to understand, it follows that this desire to understand is the one and only foundation of virtue, nor shall we desire to understand things for any other end. . . .'[3]

Part i, p. 48: 'The end of . . . rational agents considered as such, is reason or moral good. . . . This affection, like others, reaches out to its proper object, and rests in the possession of it, as its true end; whether it be, or be not, connected with happiness.'
[1] *Treatise*, ii, p. 126.    [2] *Ethics*, Part IV, Scholium to Prop. XVIII.
[3] Ibid., Part IV, Proof to Prop. XXVI. Compare Kant, *Fundamental*

We are now left with two questions: first, how will the functions and status of practical reason vary with these two views, and secondly, which view is the correct one?

In answering the first question we must recall that, granted that reasoning must be caused by a passion, we cannot hope to escape the conclusion that the last passion which causes us to reason must always be unexamined by reason. This remains true whether we accept Hume's or Spinoza's account of the nature of this passion. But if we accept Spinoza's, then the only passion which our reason is unable to examine is the passion to act rationally itself, for this is according to him the passion which causes us to act rationally, whereas, if we accept Hume's, our reason will be controlled not by a desire to act rationally as such, but by any and every desire which may happen to employ reason as a means to its fulfilment. The survey which reason makes of our passions will then never be all-inclusive, for on every given occasion some particular desire, or the desire for happiness, which called our reason to its service, will stand outside its scrutiny. Thus I may desire to go to London, and hence to reason in order to discover how to get there, but my reason will have no mandate for inquiring further whether I really want to go. Or I may desire to be happy; and hence to reason in order to discover what will make me happy, but, again, I am left without an impulse to ask whether what I really want is to promote my own happiness. I shall in fact never form a wholly adequate idea of the object of my desire, for I shall see this object adequately only within the limits imposed by some already given and unexamined desire. Whereas if I desire to reason and to act rationally for its own sake, then, although I shall not be able to examine *this* desire, yet the ideas which I form of particular actions will

*Principles of the Metaphysic of Morals* in Abbot's *Kant's Theory of Ethics*, p. 12: 'For reason recognises the establishment of a good will as its highest practical destination, and in attaining this purpose is capable of a satisfaction only of its own proper kind, namely, that from the attainment of an end, which end again is determined by reason only, notwithstanding that this may involve many a disappointment to the ends of inclination.' Also p. 47: '. . . *rational nature exists as an end in itself.*'

have a chance of becoming adequate, for the desire which prompts my reasoning in this case is the desire to act from adequate ideas itself. For to desire to act rationally for its own sake *is* to desire to inquire what I should want to do *all things* considered, whereas if I desire to use my reason only in order to fulfil some desire other than the desire to act rationally I cannot consider all things, for I cannot consider this desire. In the second case, then, even though I have used my reason I shall still be in the position which Spinoza describes of the man who does 'willy nilly things which he knows absolutely nothing about', whereas in the former case I shall be 'governed only by myself and do only those things which I know to be of primary importance for my life and which on that account I desire most'.

There remains the question: Do men desire to act rationally for its own sake? Hume, as we have seen, seems to think that they do not, whereas Spinoza thinks not merely that they happen to have this desire from time to time, but also that they must have it whenever they think about it. Hume regards this passion as negligible if not as non-existent, whereas for Spinoza it is the master passion. Which of these two views is right, and again what accounts for the discrepancy between them?

In answering this question we have, I think, first to ask whether Hume's system was really complete without the admission of a desire to act rationally for its own sake. Now if we recall the kind of functions which Hume allows to reason when it is operative, it seems at least unlikely that the reasoning which performs these functions is always brought into operation by an ulterior motive. True all the directive operations of reason are brought about in this way. When reason directs existing passions by discovering relationships of class-member, genus-species, process-constituent, and material implication, then this reasoning is always brought into operation by the desire to discover what thing is a member of a class of which some member is desired, or a species of a genus of which some species is desired, or a constituent of which the process is desired, or the material implication of an act which is desired. We desire to discover these things because of our given particular desires. But in the case of the promptive operations of reason it is not so easy to see that our desire to make judgements has always ulterior motives. What causes us to desire to take a 'distant view or reflection' and to act in accordance with it? It may of course be a desire to avoid disappointment, for we may have learnt by experience that the best way to avoid being disappointed is to think before we act. But it seems unlikely that such a desire is responsible for all inquiries which prompt action. Moreover, we observed at the end of the last chapter that Hume's system remains incomplete so long as he disregards the possibility of determining our actions by choice between adequate ideas of all actions open to us in a situation, and in order to act in this way it is necessary to be prompted by the desire to act rationally for its own sake; no mere desire not to be disappointed can cause us to form adequate ideas of all possible actions and their consequences, for it cannot cause us to form an adequate idea of being disappointed. It is true indeed that Hume does not take any account of such a comprehensive choice and that he did not do so may well have been due to his view that there is no desire to reason for its own sake, and yet this seems to be the main shortcoming of his theory of practical reason. But in order to determine whether this is a genuine shortcoming we have to ask whether he was right in not taking account of the possibility of men desiring to act rationally for its own sake.

Now here I think we have immediately to admit that it is an empirical fact that we do sometimes have such a desire. We can establish by introspection and by questioning others that men are often moved to determine themselves by adequate ideas simply for the sake of so doing. But there remains the question of whether we can go farther than this, and say that this desire is more proper to their natures than any other; that men are so constituted that they *must* desire to act rationally whenever they think about it. We have already said that Spinoza took this to be the case. For Spinoza maintains that determining ourselves by adequate ideas is constitutive of our very essence, and that hence the desire to do so is coextensive with the desire to exist:

'For us to act with absolute virtue is nothing else but to act in accordance with the dictates of reason, to live, to persist in our own essence (all of which mean the same) in seeking what is useful for us.'[1]

But Spinoza also maintains that men must desire to exist:

'That a man should from the necessity of his own nature desire not to exist or to be changed into something else, this is as impossible as that something should come out of nothing, as any one will see after a little reflection.'[2]

Now it is plain that Hume could not possibly hold this view as it stands, and he is precluded from holding it by arguments which we have fully accepted. For he has shown that propositions about desiring are causal propositions and that all causal propositions are empirical. Hence we cannot say that there is anything which must *a priori* move us when we form an adequate idea of it, not even the idea of existing. And hence Spinoza is wrong in maintaining that we can know *a priori* that we must on reflection desire to exist. But if indeed a desire to determine ourselves by adequate ideas can be shown to be coextensive with the desire to exist, then there will at least be very good empirical grounds for saying that on reflection men will have this desire; for the desire to exist is at least widespread, and, as Spinoza points out, it is logically prior to all other desires, since if we do not desire to exist at all we cannot desire any particular forms of existence such as happiness:

'No one can desire to be blessed, to act well and to live well if he does not at the same time desire to be, to act and to live, that is in fact to exist.'[3]

But are we justified in saying that the desire to act from adequate ideas is coextensive with the desire to exist? This clearly will depend upon the view we take of the self. For existence here does not refer to mere physical but to conscious existence,

[1] *Ethics*, Part IV, Prop. XXIV.    [2] Ibid., Part IV, Scholium to Prop. XX.
[3] Ibid., Part IV, Prop. XXI.

since the *esse* of man is to be rational. This is what Spinoza means by the 'conatus in suo esse perseverare'. And Spinoza maintains that in so far as we are driven about by the ideas of acts of which we have no proper knowledge and are at the mercy of circumstance, we are no proper conscious beings at all; it is only in so far as we direct our own conduct by coming to possess full knowledge of our actions that we are properly persons. It is thus that he interprets 'the wages of sin is death'.

Here is not the place to discuss the merits of this view, which would involve us in a consideration of the self and would lead us beyond the limits of this book. But if it is true, as it appears to be, that the desire to act rationally for its own sake is widely spread among humanity because rational action is constitutive of the self, then it is clear why Hume did not hold that the desire for rational action as such is a predominant one. For a mere bundle of impressions and ideas is not the kind of conscious being which constitutes itself through rational action. Such a bundle would be no more than a psychic continuum and could exist without rational action, nor is there any reason to suppose that it could have any desire to become a conscious self.

We can conclude then that, although some of the functions which Hume allows to reason seem to presuppose a desire to reason for its own sake as their cause, yet he neither did recognize the existence of such a desire nor could he have found any good reasons for saying that such a desire should exist. He might indeed have admitted it as an empirical fact, but he would not have been able to connect it with the rest of man's nature. But, granting that there is a desire to act rationally for its own sake, then the doctrine of reason as the slave of the passions would have committed Hume no longer to his depreciative view of practical reason, for whenever reason is caused by this desire it can examine all our desires, and we can act, as far as it is in our power to form them, from wholly adequate ideas. Here then is the answer to the question which we asked at the beginning of this chapter: How far are such restrictions as Hume places on the power of reason the essential consequence of his views on the nature of reason and action, and how far are they due to extraneous causes and might be abandoned without detriment to his general position? The view that reason is the mediate cause of action does indeed imply that reason is the slave of the passions, but it does not imply that reason is the slave of any passion excepting the passion to reason; all particular passions reason can control. Hume's own particular version of the slave-of-the-passions doctrine was not the necessary consequence of his views on reason and on action, but rather of his extreme empiricist theory of the self.

## REASON AND MORALITY

THE conclusions of the last chapter have brought to the end our examination of Hume's general account of the relation between reason and conduct. Our main task is therefore completed. But I think we cannot leave this subject altogether without some account of his discussion of the relation between reason and specifically *moral* conduct, for it was his concern with this latter problem which led him to embark on his inquiry into practical reason in general. Hume argued, as we saw in Chapter II, that moral conduct must be essentially dependent upon something which has the power of moving an agent to act, and hence that, if we wish to maintain that moral conduct is dependent on reason, we have first to show that reason has this power. If reason cannot be practical, then morality must in all essentials be independent of reason and rest on sense alone. Thus there remain two questions which we must attempt to answer: *first*, What conclusions about the relations between reason and morality does Hume draw from his account of practical reason? and *secondly*, Do these conclusions in fact follow from the account of practical reason which we have attributed to him?

We shall not find it easy to answer either of these questions, for Hume's treatment of the relation between reason and morality, though interesting in parts, is on the whole unconvincing. Moreover here, as elsewhere in the *Treatise*, his first statement of his position is simple and rather dogmatic, but quite unlike his last. That is not to say that he contradicts himself or eventually abandons his original view in favour of another, but rather that the detailed elaboration of his first statement both enriches and complicates it in such a way that it ends far other than it began. Moreover, in this case it is true to say that his final statement is not free from confusion and is, in the last analysis, untenable. To deal justly with the problems involved would require a separate study. I cannot here do more than summarize the kind of argument which such a work would pursue.

Now we must begin by noting that in many parts of the *Treatise* Hume's argument appears to be as follows: Moral conduct must rest on something which can move an agent to act; reason or judgement cannot move an agent to act; hence moral conduct must be independent of reason and must rest on sense alone. Thus it is that he writes:

'... the course of the argument leads us to conclude, that since vice and virtue are not discoverable merely by reason, or the comparison of ideas, it must be by means of some impression or sentiment they occasion, that we are able to mark the difference betwixt them. Our decisions concerning moral rectitude and depravity are evidently perceptions; and as all perceptions are either impressions or ideas, the exclusion of the one is a convincing argument for the other. Morality, therefore, is more properly felt than judged of; ...'[1]

If we read the *Treatise* in a cursory manner we may well think this is all that Hume has to say about the question, for this is the view which he seems to take in the early sections of Book III where he is specifically concerned with the basis of moral conduct, and he does not explicitly reopen the question later on. Moreover, I think this argument is generally accepted as representative of Hume's position, and, indeed, as his most significant contribution to moral philosophy.

But there is good reason for doubting whether Hume ever really subscribed to this naïve argument, or adhered to its conclusions without qualification. If this was his view, then he would be maintaining a position which, so far from following from his account of practical reason, would actually be incompatible with it. For the minor premiss of the argument 'Since whatever is the basis of moral conduct must move to action and, since reason cannot move to action, reason cannot be the basis of moral conduct', is not only not proved by Hume, but is flatly contradicted by him. It is true indeed he shows that *a priori* judgements can only affect conduct incidentally and not essentially; and this argument certainly precludes him from

[1] *Treatise*, ii, p. 178.

maintaining with many earlier rationalists that moral conduct rests on *a priori* judgements; for it is essential and not incidental influence which Hume assumed must be attributable to reason if it is the foundation of morality.[1] But this argument alone neither commits nor entitles him to say that moral conduct must rest on sense alone. It remains possible that it should rest on empirical reasoning, and Hume, as we have seen, does allow that empirical reasoning can be practical. Hence we cannot be content to accept the above argument. We must look farther, and examine more closely the extent to which he did finally exclude reason from influencing moral conduct.

If, with this in mind, we turn to the later sections of Book III we see at once that Hume by no means excludes reason from all influence on morality. On the contrary there are two respects in which he makes reason the *sine qua non* of moral action. For first, 'resulting from reflection and judgement' enters into his definition of approval, and approval is according to him the *ground* of all moral obligation; and, secondly, 'resulting from reflection and judgement' enters into his definition of the 'natural obligations', and the 'natural obligations' are themselves 'a species of morality'.

We have already analysed Hume's account of the natural obligations.[2] All that remains to be said of them concerns their relation to the moral obligations, and this we must leave aside until these have been considered. We have therefore next to inquire what Hume means by moral obligations; to what extent reflection and judgement are constitutive of them; and, finally, whether the role which he allots to reflection and judgement in determining these obligations is either sufficient in itself or the consistent outcome of his analysis of practical reason.

There is in the *Treatise* only one passage where Hume offers a specific definition of what it is to be morally obliged:

'All morality depends upon our sentiments; and when any action or quality of the mind pleases us *after a certain manner*, we say

---

[1] See above, Ch. IV, p. 119 f.     [2] See above, Ch. IV, p. 122 ff.

it is virtuous; and when the neglect or non-performance of it displeases us *after a like manner*, we say that we lie under an obligation to perform it.'[1]

The sum of this view is that there are certain acts which we call virtuous, and by saying that they are virtuous we mean that they are such as to occasion in us a special feeling of pleasure, a feeling which elsewhere Hume describes as approval. Moral obligations are related to the thought of virtuous acts. The idea of failing to do those acts which we approve of is itself displeasing to us, and to say that we are morally obliged is to say that we are prompted to perform an action by the peculiar displeasure we take in its omission.

In offering this interpretation of the above passage we are guilty of a slight emendation. Taken quite literally, what Hume says is not that to be obliged is *to be moved* by the displeasure which we take in the thought of omitting a virtuous act, but that we are obliged *when* we feel this displeasure. This might be interpreted to mean that being obliged is not being moved by feelings of displeasure, but that it is the feeling of displeasure itself. But plainly being obliged cannot *consist* in taking displeasure, and Hume is the last person who could have held such a view. The distinction between recognizing the virtue of an action, i.e., on his view, that it is an object of approval, and the obligation to do this action was the pivot of his argument against Clarke: 'These two particulars are evidently distinct. It is one thing to know virtue, and another to conform the will to it'; if we are to show that an action is '*obligatory*', we must 'also point out the connection betwixt [it] and the will'.[2] There can I think be no doubt that in saying we are morally obliged *when* the neglect of any action displeases us after a certain manner, Hume is merely adopting an abbreviated way of saying that we are morally obliged when we are moved by the thought of an act *because* the neglect of it displeases us after a certain manner. It is not difficult to see how he came to make this abbreviation. For he thought it a well-founded empirical fact that the thought of pleasure causes

---

[1] *Treatise*, ii, p. 220.  [2] Ibid., ii, p. 174.

desire and that of pain aversion.[1] And from this it does follow that if the thought of omitting an act displeases us, we shall, *ceteris paribus*, be moved to do the act.

We can then conclude that according to Hume to be morally obliged is to be prompted to do some act by the thought that it is an object of approval, and by our consequent displeasure in its omission.[2] From this it follows that the analysis of approval and of the terms 'virtuous', 'good', 'praiseworthy' (terms which he uses as synonymous) is for Hume of paramount importance. Once it has been granted that we are morally obliged to do acts by the thought that they are virtuous, the two questions, what constitutes virtue, and how can propositions attributing virtue be verified, become the central problems of his moral philosophy. And, indeed, it is with these questions that the later parts of the *Treatise* and most of the *Inquiry* are almost exclusively concerned. But the problem of approval as a whole is a far wider one than that of those particular cases of approval which give rise to moral obligations. We approve of many things besides acts and the character-dispositions which give rise to them; we approve, for instance, of humour and wit. For this reason the analysis of approval carries Hume far away from the problem of obligation, and we are disappointed to find that he has very little to say about the 'obligations of duty', far less in fact than about the 'obligations of interest'. Indeed, by the time we reach the end of the *Treatise* the problem of moral obligation has almost been lost to sight. It seems as though Hume had come to the conclusion that the

---

[1] See *Treatise*, ii, p. 177: 'Nothing can be more real, or concern us more, than our own sentiments of pleasure and uneasiness; and if these be favourable to virtue, and unfavourable to vice, no more can be requisite to the regulation of our conduct and behaviour.'

[2] Here it may be objected that on Hume's view moral obligation cannot consist in being moved to do an *action* by the thought that doing the action is an object of approval, since he held that actions are not properly objects of approval at all. What we approve of is not actions but the *sentiments* and *character-dispositions* which give rise to them. From this premiss it may be argued that he is committed to the view that moral obligation consists in being moved not to *do* certain acts but to *have* certain character-dispositions. Hume does at times exhibit leanings towards this kind of view, but it cannot in fairness be attributed to him. See Appendix.

main problem for the moral philosopher was to show how we come to attribute value to acts, character-dispositions, and qualities of mind, and that, since approval and disapproval are the sole *ground* of moral obligation, nothing more need be said about the latter.

With the greater part of Hume's views on virtue and approval we are not here concerned. Our problem in this chapter is the relation between reason and morality. In approval and disapproval we are interested only in so far as they give rise to moral obligations, or constitute their ground; with the further question of what gives rise to feelings of approval and whether their grounds be in sympathy or utility we are in no way concerned. This part of Hume's philosophy has been dealt with at length by T. H. Green, Ingemar Hedenius, and others. It has in fact attracted the attention of Hume's critics and commentators far more than his contribution to any other moral problem. We can leave it to these who have dealt with it so amply. But there are certain aspects of Hume's theory of approval which, since he regards approval as the ground of moral obligation, are intimately connected with his views on the relation between reason and moral conduct, and these we cannot ignore.

Now, prima facie we may well think that Hume must regard the attribution of virtue as wholly independent of reason and judgement. For being good, virtuous, praiseworthy, or a proper object of approval (characteristics which are for him synonymous) is not, according to Hume, possessing any quality which can belong to a thing independently of those who observe it. Things are not good or proper objects of approval in themselves, but because in certain circumstances we should approve of them. It is because things are objects of approval that they are good, not because they are good that they are objects of approval. Now, since the goodness of a thing is defined in terms of men's reactions to it, it might be natural to suppose that no reasoning enters into the definition of goodness. Each man, we may say, will call good that object which pleases him 'after a certain manner' when he is thinking of it, and propositions attributing goodness will have reference only to the temporary and subjective states of individual observers; they will be no more and no less corrigible than propositions about pure sense data.

There is indeed one passage in the *Treatise* which seems to support this view. In matters of valuation, Hume writes:

'. . . the opinions of men . . . carry with them a peculiar authority, and are, in a great measure, infallible. The distinction of moral good and evil is founded on the pleasure or pain which results from the view of any sentiment or character; and, as that pleasure or pain cannot be unknown to the person who feels it, it follows, that there is just so much vice or virtue in any character as everyone places in it, and that it is impossible in this particular we can ever be mistaken.'[1]

But this solitary passage is not sufficient to justify us in attributing to Hume a Boo-Hurray theory of moral valuation. For there are many passages where he asserts a contrary view, and even here where he states that we can never be mistaken about moral good and evil he qualifies this assertion in a footnote by referring the reader to a subsequent consideration of 'a right and wrong taste in morals, eloquence and beauty'. When he comes to consider this question he argues emphatically that good and evil are not 'determined merely by sentiment'. We can make value *judgements*, and these judgements are *corrigible*. To say that a thing is an object of approval is to say something essentially different from 'I' or 'many people', 'the majority', or even 'everybody' have a feeling of liking for it or are inclined to react to it with the expression 'Hurray'.

Hume distinguishes approval from mere liking on two grounds. First he defines approval as a peculiar kind of pleasure, 'that *peculiar* kind which makes us praise or condemn'. It is a feeling distinguishable from others in terms of its quality, a quality which can only be defined ostensively:

'. . . it is evident that, under the term *pleasure*, we comprehend sensations, which are very different from each other, and which have only such a distant resemblance as is requisite to make them be expressed

[1] *Treatise*, ii, p. 246.

by the same abstract term.  A good composition of music and a bottle of good wine equally produce pleasure; and, what is more, their goodness is determined merely by the pleasure.  But shall we say, upon that account, that the wine is harmonious, or the music of a good flavour?'[1]

But Hume is not satisfied with this distinction.  Just as in the case of the distinction between the calm and the violent passions he began by saying that they 'feel' different, and then went on to define them in terms of the way in which we come to have them, so here too he begins by drawing the distinction in terms of feeling quality, and then goes on to argue that feeling approval differs from mere liking in that it arises from an impartial consideration of its object:

'It is only when a character is considered in general, without reference to our particular interest, that it causes such a feeling or sentiment as denominates it morally good or evil.'[1]

This view is expressed quite unambiguously in the following passage:

'Every quality of the mind is denominated virtuous which gives pleasure by the mere survey, as every quality which produces pain is called vicious. . . . every particular person's pleasure and interest being different, it is impossible men could ever agree in their sentiments and judgements, unless they chose some common point of view, from which they might survey their object, and which might cause it to appear the same to all of them.  Now, in judging of characters, the only interest or pleasure which appears the same to every spectator, is that of the person himself whose character is examined, or that of persons who have a connection with him.  And, though such interests and pleasures touch us more faintly than our own, yet, being more constant and universal, they counterbalance the latter even in practice, *and are alone admitted in speculation as the standard of virtue and morality.  They alone produce that particular feeling or sentiment on which moral distinctions depend.*'[2]

---

[1] Ibid., p. 180.

[2] Ibid., p. 285 (my italics); see also ibid., p. 278: 'It is . . . from the influence of characters and qualities upon those who have an intercourse with any person, that we blame or praise him.  We consider not whether the persons affected by the qualities be our acquaintance or strangers, countrymen or foreigners.  Nay, we overlook our own interest in those *general judgements*, and blame not a man for opposing us in any of our pretensions, when his own interest is particularly concerned.' (My italics.)

Here Hume defines approving as having certain sentiments towards a thing as the result of considering its qualities as they are in themselves and without reference to our own particular interest. It follows that I cannot say that I approve of a thing unless I have specifically eliminated from my view of it those characteristics which it has in relation to my interests only and those distortions which it acquires by being observed from my particular standpoint in space and time. I approve of many things which would displease me if I regarded them as they affect me personally. I approve, for example, of the good qualities of an enemy, though they are harmful to me,[1] and I approve equally of similar qualities in my contemporaries and in those who lived a long time ago, though the one gives me more personal pleasure than the other.

'. . . it is evident that those sentiments [of pleasure and disgust], whence ever they are derived, must vary according to the distance and contiguity of the objects; nor can I feel the same lively pleasure from the virtues of a person who lived in Greece two thousand years ago, that I feel from the virtues of a familiar friend and acquaintance. Yet I do not say that I esteem the one more than the other; . . .'[2]

It follows from this that, despite his analysis of objects of approval in terms of the pleasurable feeling which they occasion in a spectator, Hume is very far from maintaining that '$x$ is an object of approval' means 'I have a liking for $x$ here and now'. It means '$x$ is the kind of thing which, considered without regard to the special relation in which it stands to my personal interests, arouses feelings of pleasure in me or any other disinterested spectator of like susceptibilities'. Hence approving differs from mere liking in that it is by definition a state of feeling pleasure which results from reflecting and judging,

---

[1] See *Treatise*, ii, p. 180: 'Nor is every sentiment of pleasure and pain . . . of that *peculiar* kind which makes us praise or condemn. The good qualities of an enemy are hurtful to us, but may still command our esteem and respect. It is only when a character is considered in general, without reference to our particular interest, that it causes such a feeling or sentiment as denominates it morally good or evil.'

[2] Ibid., p. 277; see also ibid., p. 278: 'Our servant, if diligent and faithful, may excite stronger sentiments of love and kindness than Marcus Brutus, as represented in history; but we say not, upon that account, that the former character is more laudable than the latter.'

i.e. from reflecting and judging concerned only with a special aspect of the object which gives pleasure.[1]

We have now to notice a further and very important point. So far we have seen only that Hume does not equate '*x* is good' and 'I like *x*'. For he relates the goodness of a thing not to liking, but to approval which is essentially different from liking. But a careful analysis of his account of goodness and approval shows also that neither does he equate '*x* is good' with 'I approve of *x*'. My approval of *x* rests on a judgement about what my feelings towards *x* *would be if* I contemplated *x* as it is in itself and independently of my relation to it. This is an empirical judgement which asserts that *x* is for me a proper object of approval. Now such a judgement may well be false, for even after reflection I may have a completely mistaken idea of the true nature of *x*, or may not have succeeded in eliminating from my idea of it the particular relation in which it stands to me. In this case it is true that my feelings for *x* will be feelings not of liking but of approval, for they will be founded on a judgement about what *x* is like irrespective of its relation to me. I shall approve of *x* and I shall *think* that *x* is good or a proper

---

[1] It is in this context particularly important to notice that it would not by any means be true to say that approving is 'liking after reflection', or that it is simply liking an object of which we have formed an adequate idea. Liking and approving are for Hume essentially different in that they are our reactions to different aspects of their objects. I like a thing when I feel pleasure as the result of regarding it without abstracting from my idea its relation to myself. I approve of it when I feel pleasure as the result of regarding it abstracted from this relation. Hence while it is true to say that I cannot approve of a thing without reflecting and judging, for without these processes I cannot see the thing independently of its relation to my interests, it does not follow that approval rests on a wholly adequate idea of its object, for an adequate idea of this would have to include its relation to me. The idea on which my approval is based is an adequate idea of its object without this relation. Moreover, it does not follow that *liking* cannot also be based on judgement. Hume in fact says nothing about this point, but plainly my liking of an object may occur either before or after I have reflected about it. I may be presented with the thought of an object which immediately produces in me feelings of pleasure, or I may have these feelings only after I have contemplated the object and formed an adequate idea of it. Hence, though Hume does differentiate between approving and liking by saying that approving rests on judgement, he cannot mean that approving rests on judgement and liking does not. It is rather that approving *must* result from reflecting and judging whereas liking may or may not. From this it follows that we may well dislike what we approve of and approve of what we dislike, and in so doing we may be behaving perfectly rationally.

object of approval (for approving of $x$ and thinking that $x$ is good are one and the same), but $x$ will not *be* good, for a fuller understanding of it would result in a change of my feelings of approval.

It is true indeed that Hume does not himself deal at any considerable length with the difference between our *genuinely* approving of a thing (as opposed to liking it) and our *rightly* approving of it (as opposed to genuinely, but mistakenly, approving). By far the greater part of his argument about the essence of goodness and approval is concerned with the difference between genuinely approving and merely liking, the way in which we mistake feelings of liking for those of approval, and how we can correct this mistake.[1] In this case he is really concerned with a verbal error; we say we approve when we really mean that we like, for here we have not even tried to see our object independently of its relation to us, while in so far as we have done this our feelings are genuine feelings of approval even though they may not be proper ones. None the less, that we do not merely sometimes fail to make moral valuations altogether, but also make false ones, does follow from Hume's whole argument. Though he did not discuss this point he clearly recognized it; for he argues that, because approval rests not on mere subjective feeling but on disinterested consideration, discussion and agreement about moral values is possible. The truth of value judgements is measured by a *standard* which is common to all men of the same susceptibility. This is a point which he makes most emphatically:

'. . . every particular man has a peculiar position with regard to others; and it is impossible we could ever converse together on any reasonable terms, were each of us to consider characters and persons only as they appear from his peculiar point of view. In order, therefore, to prevent those continual *contradictions* and arrive at a more *stable* judgement of things, we fix on some *steady* and *general* points of view, and always,

[1] See *Treatise*, ii, p. 180: 'It is true, those sentiments from interest and morals are apt to be confounded, and naturally run into one another. It seldom happens that we do not think an enemy vicious, and can distinguish betwixt his opposition to our interest and real villainy or baseness. But this hinders not but that the sentiments are in themselves distinct; and a man of temper and judgement may preserve himself from these illusions.'

in our thoughts, place ourselves in them, whatever may be our present situation. In like manner, external beauty is determined merely by pleasure; and it is evident a beautiful countenance cannot give so much pleasure, when seen at a distance of twenty paces, as when it is brought nearer us. We say not, however, that it appears less beautiful; because we *know what effect it will have in such a position, and by that reflection we correct its momentary appearance.*[1]

It is plain Hume thought that our endeavour to arrive at these 'stable judgements' might succeed in varying degrees, and that we might when 'conversing on reasonable terms' point out to each other the inadequacy of our *opinions* in the light of new evidence. The face that is *really* beautiful, the character which is *really* good, is the one in which we should take aesthetic or moral pleasure if we saw it as it really is independently of our relation to it. We know what effect the face would have if brought nearer to us, and what 'degree of affection and admiration' Marcus Brutus would call forth 'were we to approach near to that renowned patriarch'.[2] Our judgements of approval take account only of the effects which their objects would have if we saw them in a certain manner but, since we can never be sure that we are seeing them in this manner, these judgements may always be wrong.

It is usual to interpret Hume as saying that '*x* is good' means no more than 'I approve of *x*' or 'the majority approves of *x*' or 'everybody approves of *x*'. But plainly there is no need to attribute to him this very unplausible view. On his premises, an object may *be* good even though nobody has ever *thought* it good, and even though the majority, or even everybody, has always *thought* it bad. For its goodness is defined by him not in terms of the feelings of approval which it *actually* arouses, but in terms of the feelings which it *would* arouse in a perfectly disinterested spectator who formed a perfect idea of it. And it may be that nobody has ever formed a perfectly adequate

---

[1] Ibid., p. 277–8 (Hume's italics in the middle, mine at the end).

[2] Ibid., p. 278; see also p. 279: 'We blame equally a bad action which we read of in history, with one performed in our neighbourhood the other day; the meaning of which is, that we *know from reflection* that the former action *would* excite as strong sentiments of disapprobation as the latter, were it placed in the same position.' (My italics.)

idea of an object irrespective of its relation to him, and hence that nobody has ever as yet been right in thinking that any object is good. In fact in order to know that an object is good the knower would need to be omniscient, for he would need perfect insight into the nature of the object and all its effects. Hence what we or even the majority of people think to be an object of approval need not necessarily be one.[1]

This, of course, is not to say that Hume ever regarded goodness as an objective quality pertaining to actions and characters independently of the experient's attitude towards them. Approval is, for him, *formally* dependent on judgement; *materially* it depends on sensibility. Hence, in so far as the susceptibilities of rational beings vary, the proper as well as the actual objects of approval will be different for different people. Only in so far as men's susceptibilities are alike, while their knowledge of possible objects of approval and their ability to abstract from their own interests vary, will the variations in their valuations be due to ignorance and error and be capable of emendation. The goodness of characters and actions remains for Hume essentially relative to the feelings which their contemplation is able to raise in the observer. But it is not relative to every passing whim, but only to those feelings which

---

[1] This interpretation of Hume is contrary to that offered by Professor Broad in *Five Types of Ethical Theory*. There Professor Broad maintains that although '*x* is good' means for Hume something more than 'I approve of *x* here and now', yet it does not mean more than that the majority of people approve of it. Although Hume implies that we can argue about the goodness of a thing, this argument is always about a historical fact, namely how many people have approved of *x*. Such an argument is, Broad thinks, 'utterly irrelevant' to this kind of question, and he concludes that Hume's theory must be wrong.

See *Five Types of Ethical Theory*, p. 85: 'Hume's theory is that "*x* is good" means that the contemplation of *x* will call forth an emotion of approval in all or most men on all or most occasions. Such statements as this can be argued about and supported or refuted by observation and collection of statistics.' Also p. 115: '. . . the logical consequence of Hume's theory is not that in disputes on moral questions there comes a point beyond which we can only say "*de gustibus non est disputandum*". The logical consequence of his theory is that all such disputes *could* be settled, and that the way to settle them is to collect statistics of how people do in fact feel. And to me this kind of answer seems utterly irrelevant to this kind of question. If I am right in this, Hume's theory must be false.'

I do think that this is an exceedingly uncharitable, if not a completely false, interpretation of what Hume says.

would be forced upon any disinterested observer of the same nature by an adequate contemplation of the objects on which he passes judgement. Thus in Hume's view it is only in so far as human nature is basically uniform that what is of value for one must also be of value for another, and that we can speak of things being good without specifying for whom. In so far as our susceptibilities are genuinely different, the divergencies between our valuations are fundamental and ultimate, and cannot be affected either by further contemplation or by discourse and persuasion. Hence Hume can hold both that in matters of moral value our feelings and sentiments are the ultimate court of appeal, and at the same time that there is 'a right and wrong taste in morals', the wrong taste being corrigible by judgement.[1]

It is not surprising that Hume should take this view of moral valuation. It is a view perfectly consistent with his account of the relation between reason and the affections which pervades the whole of the *Treatise*. In the calm passions, the artificial virtues, the moral and aesthetic valuations, we find the same conception of natural passions and affections corrected by reflection and judgement. It is true that this general conception

---

[1] Thus Hume's view that there may well be ultimate differences in our attribution of goodness does not entail in moral values *de gustibus non est disputandum*. For, since goodness is not defined by him in absolute terms, when I attribute goodness to a thing I *mean* that it is a proper object of approval for some particular person or persons. Hence when we dispute about the goodness of *x* we are not considering whether what is really good for you must also be really good for me, but whether *x* is really good for me. To say that, if I think that *x* is a proper object of approval and you do not, there can be neither argument nor agreement between us, is like saying that if I desire to go to the cinema and you to go on the river I cannot discuss with you whether you really want to go on the river and you cannot argue with me about whether I really want to go to the pictures. About these things we can argue and agree even though our desiring natures may be so different that we never in any circumstances want to do the same thing.

It must not be assumed from these arguments that I am in any way agreeing with Hume's definition of good. It seems plain that even though Hume may be right in saying that being a proper object of approval is one meaning of the term 'good', it is at least not the only meaning. Even Hume takes this view, for among the reasons why we approve of things he includes their goodness, using goodness in the sense that they are conducive to the well-being of mankind.

only emerges gradually as the second and third books of the
*Treatise* proceed, and there is throughout an undercurrent of
a more negative view towards the practical power of reason;
but the farther we advance the less hesitant Hume becomes
about this power, and the more does he seem to proceed from
the merely negative assertion that reason *alone* cannot control
the affections to the positive conception of reason as their
*mediate cause.* He is at his most hesitant in the sections on the
calm passions. Here he says much about the theoretical judgements which are the basis of the calm passions, judgements
about the intrinsic nature of possible objects of desire, but
nothing, except by implication, about the practical judgements
which conclude our reflection, judgements about what we must
be moved to do in view of the nature of these objects.[1] He is
much more positive when he comes to write about the artificial
virtues, for here he definitely allows that our passions are influenced by practical as well as by theoretical judgements.
The 'judgement and understanding provide the remedy for
what is incommodious in the affections'.[2] But I think we can
say that Hume is most positive about the practical power of
reason in the sections which we have just been considering.
Moral values, like the artificial virtues, are defined as feelings
which result from reflection and judgement, and the judgements on which they rest are plainly practical. They are not
simply judgements about the nature of possible objects of
valuation, but judgements about what we *should* feel if we viewed
these objects in a special way. Our inquiries into the nature of
these objects are made with the special end of arriving at the
kind of feelings which we call approval, and the judgement that
*x* is a proper object of approval is a practical judgement—not
of course in the sense that it determines my desire or my action,
but in the sense that it determines my feelings of approval.

It will be remembered that the judgements with which Hume
was concerned in writing of the artificial virtues were directive
judgements, and the judgements with which he was concerned
in the calm passions were promptive ones. The judgements

[1] See above, Ch. IV, p. 132 f.          [2] See above, Ch. IV, p. 121 f.

which are the basis of the artificial virtues direct existing passions, whereas those which are the basis of the calm passions prompt new ones. Now we have said that it is a matter of extreme importance in determining Hume's attitude to practical reason as a whole to discover whether he allows that both directive and promptive judgements can be practical. It is evident he allows that directive judgements can be practical, for such are the foundations of the laws of nature. But we have said it is less plain whether he allows that promptive judgements can be practical, for the possibility of these judgements we could only infer from the sections on the calm passions. In view of this fact, his account of moral valuation makes an important contribution to his theory of practical reason in general, for the practical judgements which determine our moral valuations are promptive and not directive since they are all about the feelings which we should have towards *x* if we considered it in a certain way, and these are judgements which prompt feelings. It is therefore of special interest here, that, in writing of moral valuations, Hume himself refers back to his arguments about the calm passions, saying that the reasoning in both cases is the same, and making it plain that what he said about moral values was what he meant to say about the calm passions. The attempts of reason to correct our values, may not, he writes, be 'altogether efficacious', and he adds:

'Here we are contented with saying, that reason requires such an impartial conduct, but that it is seldom we can bring ourselves to it, and that our passions do not readily follow the determination of our judgement. This language will be easily understood, if we consider what we formerly said concerning that *reason* which is able to oppose our passion, and which we have found to be nothing but a general calm determination of the passions, founded on some distant view or reflection.'[1]

The reason which 'demands such an impartial conduct' is practical, i.e. it is concerned with what on consideration we should value, and it is also promptive. From this we can infer that had Hume returned to rewrite the sections on the

[1] *Treatise*, ii, p. 279.

calm passions he would have been more positive in allowing that judgements which determine these also are practical. Here we might remember that the sections on the calm passions occur in Book II, which was published a year earlier than the book which contains his account of the artificial virtues and the moral values.

We are now in a position to see what part Hume allowed to reason in determining moral conduct. It is plain from what we have said about his conception of moral obligation and his views on virtue or goodness that he did not regard our moral obligations as wholly undetermined by reason. For he has said that our being morally obliged depends upon our being moved by some special motive, and he has specified this motive as a desire to do an act because it is an object of approval and its omission an object of disapproval. But we cannot approve or disapprove of anything without considering what feelings it would evoke in us if we considered it adequately as it is in abstraction from our personal interests. Hence we can be morally obliged only as the result of some reflection and judgement. No beings are capable of having moral obligations unless they are also capable of making value judgements and submitting themselves to that 'impartial conduct required by reason'. A person unable or unwilling to distinguish between his personal interest in any act and its value, virtue or goodness, could never be moved by the thought of its value, virtue or goodness; and hence he would *ex hypothesi* be devoid of all sense of moral obligation. We cannot know what acts are our obligations without first knowing what acts are good, and we cannot know what acts are good without contemplation and judgement. Hence our sense of moral obligation is not seated in our appetitive nature alone, but in our appetitive and rational natures joined.

We may well ask whether, having made this admission, Hume has not contradicted himself. He often asserts that our being morally obliged does not depend on our reason, and yet he argues that it depends on a special motive which could not exist without reason. But in fact this is no contradiction.

Hume can maintain that approval rests on contemplation and judgement, and obligation on approval, without being, for that reason, committed to the view that obligation itself rests *essentially* and *directly* on judgement. For to approve is not in itself to be moved to do those things which we approve of, and Hume can still argue that our being so moved is independent of reason and rests on sense alone. It is true we cannot be obliged without reasoning, but this reasoning is concerned only with the *grounds* on which we are morally obliged and not with our being obliged itself. In approving I recognize that a possible act would be of a certain kind, i.e. such as to call forth feelings of approval, but this does not in itself entail any reactions on the part of my desiring nature. It is still 'one thing to know virtue' (i.e. to approve correctly) and 'another to conform the will to it'; and it is this conforming of the will, the actual desiring to do the acts which we approve of, which constitutes our sense of moral obligation, and here, Hume seems to say, reason can play no part.

This position becomes plain when we consider that value judgements, although practical in relation to our feeling approval, are still theoretical in relation to our feeling desire. The judgement 'if I contemplated *x* I should approve of *x*' is practical in relation to my approving of *x*, I cannot make this judgement without coming to feel approval; but it is quite theoretical in relation to my desiring to do *x*. 'Smelling this rose is an act which I must approve of on reflection' would, in relation to my desiring to smell this rose, be of precisely the same status as the judgement 'smelling this rose would cause me to have delectable olfactory sensations'. Both these judgements assert that the act of smelling this rose would have a certain property and neither is in any way concerned with the relation between this act and my will. It is true that if I make these judgements I shall often feel desire as a result of having made them; but it is, at least, possible to argue that whether or not I shall come to feel this desire depends simply on the fact that I am aware of the content of these judgements, and not in turn on any further mental processes. My desire to do the act will then arise merely impulsively, i.e. upon the mere thought that it would be an act of a certain kind, as a desire to eat an apple or to drink some lemonade may arise upon the thought that eating the apple will be sweet or drinking the lemonade refreshing.

Hence Hume's arguments about approval do not in themselves alone commit him to the view that our sense of moral obligation rests on reason. They commit him only to saying that we cannot act morally without first acquiring certain information (information about what we should value) which we can acquire only by making judgements. He could still argue that whether or not, having acquired this information, we shall be morally obliged, i.e. whether we shall be affected by this information, is independent of reason and rests on sense alone.

It appears likely that this was Hume's view; and yet so far from being implied by his general account of the relation between reason and action it is actually inconsistent with it. For when we consider his views on practical reason together with his theory of moral obligation and approval we must conclude that consistently he should have allowed to reason a greater part in determining our moral obligations than he in fact does. For he should have allowed to reason not only the power of mediately determining our feelings of approval but also that of mediately determining our being moved to do those acts which we approve of.

For Hume admits that we are not *always* moved *ipso facto* to do these acts,

'A house may displease me by being ill contrived for the convenience of the owner; and yet I may refuse to give a shilling towards the rebuilding of it. Sentiments must *touch the heart* to make them control our *passions*: but they need not extend *beyond the imagination*, to make them influence our *taste*.'[1]

[1] *Treatise*, ii, p. 281 (my italics). It may perhaps be thought that this passage conflicts with that quoted above, page 168. But I do not really think this is the case. For *first* Hume's assertion that we are always moved to do pleasant acts by the thought of them is only an empirical generalization, and *secondly* even though it may in fact be the case that when we contemplate adequately the thought of pleasant acts we are always moved to do them, yet without such contemplation the thought of them may remain altogether dissociated from our

This is a confirmation of what we said in Chapter IV, where we argued that theoretical judgements about the nature of an act may fail to move us even though we are intrinsically capable of being moved by them. This may happen, as we saw, because we may be aware of the nature of an action without contemplating adequately the thought of our doing it. We may fail to ask ourselves the question, 'Considering that this is an act of the kind $x$, should I be moved by the thought of it if I gave the matter my prolonged and undivided attention?' It is when we do not ask and answer this question that the thought of an action intrinsically capable of moving us may leave us indifferent. Thus Hume is right in saying that the mere knowledge that an act is an object of approval may fail 'to touch the heart' and to 'control the passions' although what is an object of approval is pleasing and what is pleasing is capable of raising desire. But Hume fails to explain how this state of affairs can arise. He does not here realize that the disparity between our knowledge and our reactions to it may be due to inattention, and that the gap could be bridged by reflection and judgement. And yet we have seen that in other places he allows for precisely this sort of control of the affections by reason. He allows for it when he states that reflection and judgement can show that it is a 'rule' or 'law' for us to respect property and contracts in view of our general well-being,[1] or when he states, as we have just seen, how they can show that we should have to feel approval for some actions if we considered disinterestedly their general utility. Acts which are in our own interest often leave us unmoved until we have judged that since they are in our interest we must desire to do them. And we do not have feelings of approval at all without inquiring what we should have to approve of if we considered the matter. Thus our behaviour in matters of interest, and our feelings of approval, can be

desiring nature. We can approve of acts without ever considering them as ones which we might possibly do and without relating them to our capacity for being affected by the thought of them. (See above, Chapter IV, p. 109 f.) Moreover, even when we do desire to do acts which we approve of in themselves we may desire more to do alternative acts which give us pleasure of some other kind. [1] See above, Ch. IV, p. 125 f.

affected by practical judgements; and it follows that, consistently, Hume should allow that our behaviour in matters of morals also can be so affected. We are not *always* moved by theoretical judgements alone even though these judgements assert that possible acts would be good or virtuous, and if reason *can* intervene in some such cases it must be able to do so here also.

Granting that Hume should have admitted that our sense of moral obligation can itself be mediately caused by reflection and judgement, we can go on to ask whether he is not also committed to saying that reflection and judgement are in some sense *constitutive* of our being morally obliged. So far nothing has been said that implies such a view. We have only shown that Hume should have said that sometimes it is our reason which mediately causes us to have moral obligations, but, in spite of this, he might still maintain that we are often obliged without any practical judgement. For he defines being morally obliged in terms of being moved by the thought that a possible act is of a certain kind (i.e. that it is good or virtuous), and in accordance with this view he would have to say that our being morally obliged is constituted by the fact that we are moved to do acts of this kind: it is irrelevant whether we come to be moved in this way as the result of reflection and judgement or by mere impulse. It merely so happens that reflection and judgement is sometimes a mediate cause not only of our approving of acts but also of our feeling obliged to do them; the fact that it is such does not make it constitutive of moral obligation.

But whether even this position could be maintained is very questionable. For once we have allowed that our sense of moral obligation itself can depend on reason, we can go on to argue that we are morally obliged only when we are moved to do virtuous acts as the result of reflection and judgement. It is true of course that, even when we are moved to do these acts impulsively, they are still good or virtuous acts, and in being moved to do them we are moved to act virtuously; but to be moved to act virtuously cannot be the same as to be morally obliged. For plainly being obliged, though a species of being moved, is not simply being moved, and the difference between being simply moved and being morally obliged cannot be accounted for solely in terms of *what* it is we are moved to do. We must be moved in a *special way* and not merely by the thought of a *special thing*. In common usage, the expression 'I am obliged to do *x*' or 'I ought to do *x*' is equated with the expression 'it is imperative for me to do *x*' or 'I must do *x*'. But it is not true that I *must* do *x* when I am impulsively moved to do it. If I am moved impulsively then I am not aware of any kind of necessity to act, and I do not experience anything which could possibly be called an obligation; for I never hesitate in what I am doing, and, no matter what special kind of act it is, I am not justified in saying more than that I *want* to do it. I can only say that I *must* do *x*, or that I am *obliged* to do *x*, when I am moved as the result of reflection and judgement, i.e. when I have asked and answered the question 'is *x* the kind of thing which I should have to be moved to do if I considered it with prolonged and undivided attention?' In this case I am aware, not simply that I want to do *x* but that in some sense I have *no other alternative*. It is only then that any awareness of mustness or obligation can arise.[1]

Now oddly enough Hume did take this view when he considered the 'natural obligations'. There he specifically argued that we are obliged only when we are moved to do what is in our interest as the result of reflection and judgement. Natural obligations are always the product of 'artifice'. Simply to be moved by the thought of what is in our interest is not to be obliged at all. But consistently with this he should have made reason constituent of the 'moral obligations' also. For otherwise it cannot possibly be said that the moral and natural obligations are both species of obligation at all, and 'obligation' used in these two cases would have no common connotation. What makes the 'natural obligations' 'natural' is that they are acts to which we are moved by the thought that they are in our own interest, and what makes them obligations is that we are

[1] See W. D. Falk, 'Morals without Faith', *Philosophy*, April 1944.

so moved as the result of making practical judgements (i.e. that they are laws or imperatives). Their obligatoriness is defined in terms of their *form*, their naturalness in terms of their *matter* or *content*. Similarly then what makes the moral obligations *moral* is that they are acts to which we are moved by the thought that they are objects of approval; but what makes them *obligations*? To this Hume gives no answer. But, plainly, if 'obligation' is to be used in the same sense in both contexts, and evidently it is, the answer should again be that they are obligations because our being moved in this case too results from reflection and judgement. The obligatoriness of the moral obligations also must be formally defined, while their morality must depend on their matter or content. For both kinds of obligations must have something in common in virtue of which they are called obligations, and something in which they differ in virtue of which they are called natural and moral. What they have in common can only be their form, and that in which they differ their content.

Hence we can say that Hume's account of practical reason together with his definition of moral obligation should force him to modify this definition. He should say that we are morally obliged when and only when we are prompted to do what we approve of as the result of realizing that we must be so prompted because we approve of it.

If Hume had taken this view he would have defined moral obligation partly in terms of being moved as a result of making practical judgements and partly in terms of the specific content of these judgements. But even this modified view would have an odd implication. For Hume would then allow that of some acts we can say we must feel moved to do them on reflection, or that we are obliged to do them in view of their conduciveness to our personal good, and of others that we must feel moved to do them on reflection, or that we are obliged to do them, in view of their being objects of approval; and we are morally obliged when we are necessitated to do acts for the latter reason. But we may well come into situations in which we are confronted with two incompatible courses of action, one of

which we find ourselves obliged to follow by the thought that
it is conducive to our own good, the other by the thought that
it is virtuous. A daughter of ailing parents may find herself
'naturally obliged' to leave home for the sake of achieving her
own good in marriage or a career, and at the same time she
may find herself 'morally obliged' to stay at home for the sake
of doing what she approves of in abstraction from her own
interest. How could this conflict be resolved? Only by asking:
Which of these two courses of action, each of which I am obliged
to follow on its own account, is the one which I must adopt on
reflection in preference to the other? When I have asked and
answered this question I have an obligation which is neither
'natural' nor 'moral' but something third. For my real duty
would consist in what I must feel moved to do *on the whole*,
though it may sometimes coincide with my 'moral' obligations,
at others it may coincide with my 'natural' ones. 'Moral' and
'natural' obligations are therefore relegated to the status of mere
prima-facie duties, my real duty being distinct from either.
But if this is so, then is it still possible to identify 'moral obligation' with those prima-facie duties which have their ground in
approval? Such an identification would contravene common
usage. For it would imply that it would in some circumstances
be our real duty, or our duty on the whole, to act contrary to
our moral obligations. We do normally think that our real and
moral duties are one and the same and that it is impossible we
can ever be morally obliged to do one thing, and yet find on
comparing it with an alternative course of action that we have
on reflection to do another. It is sheer sophistry to say that our
moral duties are a special class of prima-facie duties which it
may or may not be our duty to fulfil.

This difficulty arises on the view which Hume actually holds
just as on the hypothetical view which we have been considering. He is aware of it, and yet he raises it only to dismiss it as
a problem with which the philosopher is incompetent to deal:

'Should it be asked, *what proportion these two species of morality bear
to each other*? I would answer, that this is a question to which we can
never give any precise answer; nor is it possible to reduce to numbers

the proportion which we ought to fix betwixt them. One may safely affirm, that this proportion finds itself without any art or study of men. . . . The practice of the world goes further in teaching us the degrees of our duty, than the most subtle philosophy which was ever yet invented.'[1]

From this passage it is evident that Hume did think it our duty to conform sometimes with our moral and sometimes with our natural obligations; his reference to the 'degrees of our duty' can have no other meaning. But what about the relation between the two kinds of obligation? All he says is that 'practice goes further in teaching us the degrees of our duty, than the most subtle philosophy which was ever yet invented', i.e. that it is practice rather than theory which enables us to discover what *really* is our duty. But plainly this is not saying enough. It may indeed be true that it is from experience we learn what acts really are our duties, i.e. that experience determines the answers we give to the question: 'Which act ought I to do, the one which is my moral or the one which is my natural obligation?' But to say this is not to solve the problem of the nature of real duty or duty on the whole. Experience could only help us to discover our real duties, but of what it is to be a real duty Hume gives no indication. Yet the lines along which he should have attempted to answer this question are plain. To have a real duty can only consist in being moved to do an act as the result of prolonged and attentive consideration of all the acts

---

[1] *Treatise*, ii, p. 267. We have to note here that Hume does think that we have a moral duty to perform our natural obligations. See ibid., ii, p. 234: 'Upon the whole, then we are to consider this distinction betwixt justice and injustice, as having two different foundations, viz. that of *interest*, when men observe that it is impossible to live in society without restraining themselves by certain rules; and that of *morality*, when this interest is once observed, and men receive a pleasure from the view of such actions as tend to the peace of society, and an uneasiness from such as are contrary to it.' It may perhaps be thought that this solves the above problem, but in fact this is not the case. It is true Hume says that we approve of doing acts which are our natural obligations and hence they become moral obligations as well, but after they are natural obligations they become moral obligations only when we have already formed habits of acting in these ways. In the early stages they rest on interest only and at that stage they may well conflict with moral obligations. That Hume did not regard the fact that the natural obligations become moral ones as solving the problem of the relation between the two is shown from his admission of this problem in the passage quoted above.

which it would be possible for us to do in a given situation. For only then should we be committed to do an action in a manner which allows us no other alternative. We have a duty whenever we are moved as the result of making an all-inclusive practical judgement; and the act which we find we must do when we make this judgement will be our duty whatever *kind* of act it may turn out to be. The essence of the moral motive is determined solely by the formal conditions which bring it into existence. As soon as we try to introduce any particular content or object into its definition the rational necessity which pertains to it is qualified, and it becomes again a mere prima-facie duty.

This criticism of Hume's theory of moral obligation is only offered tentatively; it is intended to be suggestive rather than assertive, and much elaboration would be needed in order to substantiate its positive implications. But, in so far as my suggestions are accepted, one general conclusion follows. It is commonly assumed that Hume's account of the relation between reason and action commits him to saying that moral conduct is altogether independent of reason. In fact, the reverse is true. It is precisely his views on practical reason which should have enabled, and indeed did logically commit him, to say that moral conduct does depend on reason. Once he has admitted that *reflection and judgement can be the mediate cause of action*, he is irrevocably pushed nearer and nearer to maintaining that our sense of moral obligation not only can but must be determined by the practical power of reason. But the kind of moral rationalism to which Hume paves the way is different from that which the older moralists maintained. The view that our duties depend on reason alone Hume has utterly destroyed. They are indeed dependent upon practical judgements, but such judgements can only be empirical. What they assert depends materially on the natural dispositions of the agents about whom they are made, and, hence, what it is rational or a duty to do remains essentially conditioned by the empirical nature of man.

# APPENDIX

FREQUENTLY in the *Treatise* and even more often in the *Inquiry* Hume advances the argument that it is not, strictly speaking, actions that we approve of but the character-dispositions which give rise to them. True he argues that these dispositions are only approved of on account of the actions to which they normally give rise, as, for instance, a benevolent disposition is approved of because it normally gives rise to acts which promote the well-being of others. None the less, it is not the isolated actions which are approved of, but the permanent disposition of an agent to do such acts; a disposition of which the single acts are only a sign.[1] A man who fails to do good acts will be displeased with himself not so much because of his failure to do any given particular action as because of his failure to exhibit in his action a permanent disposition to do acts of this kind.

From this peculiar view Hume draws an odd yet inevitable conclusion concerning moral obligation. 'No action', he argues, 'can be required of us as our duty, unless there be implanted in human nature some actuating passion or motive capable of producing the action'. Yet 'this motive cannot be the sense of duty':[2] '. . . *no action can be virtuous, or morally good, unless there be in human nature some motive to produce it distinct from the sense of its morality.*'[3] In order to do my duty I must indeed be moved by the thought of *what* it is my duty to do; but what moves me to do it cannot be the thought *that* it is my duty. This view is in itself very surprising, yet it follows consistently from Hume's premiss that only character-dispositions and not the acts to which they give rise are objects of approval and disapproval; for, in so far as this is the case, my duty must consist in acting from certain dispositions or sentiments and not merely in effecting certain actions; and

[1] See *Treatise*, ii, p. 272: 'If any *action* be either virtuous or vicious, it is only a sign of some quality or character. It must depend upon durable principles of the mind, which extend over the whole conduct, and enter into the personal character. Actions themselves, not proceeding from any constant principle, have no influence on love or hatred, pride or humility; and consequently are never considered in morality.

'This reflection is self-evident, and deserves to be attended to, as being of the utmost importance in the present subject. We are never to consider any single action in our inquiries concerning the origin of morals, but only the quality or character from which the action proceeded. . . . Actions are indeed better indications of a character than words, or even wishes and sentiments; but it is only so far as they are such indications that they are attended with love or hatred, praise or blame.' See also p. 280.

[2] Ibid., p. 221.     [3] Ibid., p. 185.

from this it follows that we cannot do our duty from a sense of duty alone, but only from a natural disposition which it is our duty to follow.

'For it is a plain fallacy to say, that a virtuous motive is requisite to render an action honest, and, at the same time, that a regard to the honesty is the motive of the action. We can never have a regard to the virtue of an action, unless the action be antecedently virtuous. No action can be virtuous, but so far as it *proceeds from a virtuous motive. A virtuous motive, therefore, must precede the regard* to the virtue; and it is impossible that the virtuous motive and the regard to the virtue can be the same.'[1]

Hume, however, allows that on certain occasions a sense of duty may cause an action on its own account. A man who has no feelings of gratitude in his heart may yet act gratefully from a sense of duty alone. He will disapprove of himself as a person lacking in that grateful disposition of which he approves; and though the thought of his defect cannot make him obliged to act from a disposition which he does not possess, yet it can oblige him to do what he would have done from this disposition in order that he may acquire it, or at least disguise to himself, as much as possible, his want of it'.[2] In this case the act is caused by a sense of duty alone.

Such a view of the relation between obligation and approval is not very satisfactory. At the best it is very complicated and at the worst it is untenable. It would be untenable if we interpreted it to mean that since we cannot approve of actions but only of character-dispositions, our duty is not simply to do those actions which normally spring from character-dispositions we approve of but actually to act from these dispositions. For plainly it is impossible to exhibit in action dispositions which we do not possess at the time of acting. It seems, however, that such an interpretation is unwarranted, for Hume himself

[1] Ibid. 186 (my italics).

[2] See ibid., p. 185: 'But may not the sense of morality or duty produce an action, without any other motive? I answer, it may: but this is no objection to the present doctrine. When any virtuous motive or principle is common in human nature, a person who feels his heart devoid of that motive, may hate himself upon that account, and may perform the action without the motive, from a certain sense of duty, in order to acquire, by practice, that virtuous principle, or at least to disguise to himself, as much as possible, his want of it. A man that really feels no gratitude in his temper, is still pleased to perform grateful actions, and thinks he has, by that means, fulfilled his duty. . . . But though, on some occasions, a person may perform an action merely out of regard to its moral obligation, yet still this supposes in human nature some distinct principles, which are capable of producing the action, and whose moral beauty renders the action meritorious.'

argues that 'it is certain we can no more change our sentiments than the motions of the heavens'. In fact he never does maintain that we are obliged to act from motives which we do not possess, but only that we are obliged to act *as if* we possessed them; i.e. if we do possess them, to act in accordance with them and thus preserve them, and, if we do not, to try to acquire them by doing the kind of acts to which they normally give rise. Thus the argument that moral obligation, though grounded in approval, is not grounded in approval of the *acts* which we are obliged to do, but of the dispositions which give rise to them, can be maintained as long as it is not interpreted as meaning that we are obliged to act from motives which we have not got. None the less it is an exceedingly tortuous view and we may well think that Hume could have avoided it. For, in accordance with this view, he must describe the fact that $x$ is an obligation in the following manner: '$x$ is an act which is normally caused by and is a sign of character-disposition $y$, and I take pleasure in the thought of the existence of $y$ and displeasure in the thought of its non-existence, and consequently I take pleasure in the thought of the occurrence of $x$ which is a sign of $y$ and displeasure in the thought of its non-occurrence, and when I am moved to do $x$ by this feeling of displeasure I am morally obliged to do $x$.'

Granted that we approve of sentiments and character-dispositions, and that sometimes we approve of the acts to which they give rise as a sign of them, there is no reason for not admitting that sometimes we approve simply of the acts themselves. When I see a man giving away money I may approve of the act because I take it as a sign that he is a kind and generous man, but I may also approve of the act itself either on its own account or because it has an effect which I approve of. It follows that, though I may sometimes be moved to do acts by the thought that I would like other people as well as myself to be kind and generous people, I may also be moved by the thought that I disapprove of the omission of such acts in itself. Moreover it seems very odd to argue, as Hume sometimes does, that we approve of character-dispositions on account of the consequences of the actions to which they give rise, and yet to deny that these actions and their consequences are themselves objects of approval. In fact Hume frequently adopts the simpler view, and speaks of acts themselves as objects of approval, and of moral obligations as arising from our approval of them. This is the view which he takes where he defines moral obligation,[1] as well as in many other places.

Thus we are I think entitled to maintain that Hume does hold, though perhaps not quite consistently, the view of obligation which we have

[1] See above, p. 166.

attributed to him. For sometimes he maintains simply that to be obliged is to be moved to do an action by the thought that it is an object of approval, and its omission an object of disapproval; and sometimes he maintains the more complex view that to be obliged is to be moved to preserve, or acquire, through our actions, character-dispositions which we approve of, or to act as if we had these dispositions. In either case we are obliged to do actions, and not to have motives for acting.

# INDEX

*A priori* judgements: influence on action, can be indirect, 61–4, 71; cannot be direct, 66–71, 73–84; moral judgements *a priori* (17th cent.), 7–14, (18th cent.), 26–36; not *a priori* (Hume), 41–59.

Action: influenced by theoretical *a priori* judgements, 61–4, 71; by theoretical empirical judgements, 100–14; by practical judgements, 122–9; by judgements deduced from empirical premisses, 85–97; not influenced directly by *a priori* judgements, 66–71, 73–84; Hume's account of nature and causes of, 104–6; defined by Hobbes, 106 n. 2; caused by adequate and inadequate ideas, 111–14, 133–7, 158–63; whether object of approval, 168 n. 2, 190–3.

Adequate and inadequate ideas, 111–14, 133–7, 158–63.

Approval: the ground of virtue, 167; dependent on observer, 169, 176; rests on judgement, 170–2; compared with 'calm passions' and 'artificial virtues', 177–80; distinguished from liking, 171–3, 173 n. 1; '*x* is approved of' distinguished from '*x* is good', 173–6; what things can be objects of, 168 n. 2, 190–3; not always sufficient to influence action, 181–4.

*Aquinas, Thomas*, 2.

*Aristotle*, 89 n. 1.

'Artificial virtues', 122–9; compared with 'calm passions' and 'approval', 177–80; *see also* 'Natural obligations'.

*Bacon, Francis*, 116 n. 2.

*Balguy, John*, 15 n. 2, 17 n. 1, 19 n. 1, 23, 156 n. 2.

*Bayle, Pierre*, 3.

*Broad, Professor C. D.*, 176 n. 1.

*Butler, Joseph*, 36–8.

'Calm and indolent judgements of the understanding', 70, 71.

'Calm passions': analysis of, 132–7, 141–8; founded on 'distant view or reflection', 132–7, 142, 143–4; conducive to 'greatest possible good', 143, 144, 145–7; whether determination by alternative to determination by reason, 143–52; compared with 'artificial virtues' and 'approval', 177–80.

Cambridge Platonists, 11.

Character-dispositions the objects of approval, 168 n. 2, 190–3.

Choice, 86, 90–1, 139, 187–9.

*Chubb, Thomas*, 19 n. 1.

*Clarke, John* (Master of Grammar School, Hull), 19, 20–4, 34–7, 44.

*Clarke, John* (Samuel's brother), 19 n. 1.

*Clarke, Samuel*, 15 n. 2, 16–35, 42–57, 60, 67–8, 71–3, 82, 85, 119, 167.

Class-member practical judgements, 85, 86–8, 94.

Common notions, 5, 11–12.

Constituent-process practical judgements, 85, 89–90, 93.

*Cudworth, Ralph*, 11 n. 3.

*Cumberland, Richard*, 7 n. 1, 11 n. 1, 13, 15–16.

Desire, *see* Passions.

Disjunctive practical judgements, 86, 90–1.

Duty, *see* Obligation.

DATE DUE